About the Author

Dr Robin K. Mathew is a psychologist and ethnographer, renowned for his deep insights into social psychology and extensive contributions across various media platforms. Spanning the globe, he has engaged with individuals from nearly 90 different nationalities, each representing a mosaic of socio-economic, ethnic, and linguistic backgrounds.

With academic qualifications and working experience in diverse fields such as information technology, human resource management, psychology, cyber forensics, and cyber psychology, Dr Mathew has collaborated with prestigious organisations including the University of Toronto, Best Buy, The Indian Institute of Management, ICFAI Business School, the Royal Bank of Canada, and Michigan University. This extensive exposure has nurtured a deep understanding of human behaviour across varied contexts.

Over the past twelve years, Dr Mathew's prolific writing has graced numerous prestigious magazines in India and abroad. He has authored nearly 500 articles spanning a wide spectrum of subjects, each infused with the wisdom and insights garnered from his work. Additionally, Dr Mathew is a successful author with fourteen published books, each offering a unique exploration of human psychology and the complexities of the human condition.

THE HUMAN ALGORITHM

Cyberpsychology for the Digital Age

DR ROBIN K. MATHEW

HAY HOUSE

HAY HOUSE INDIA
New Delhi • London • Sydney
Carlsbad, California • New York City

Hay House Publishers (India) Pvt Ltd
Muskaan Complex, Plot No. 3, B-2, Vasant Kunj, New Delhi – 110070, India

Hay House LLC, P.O. Box 5100, Carlsbad, CA 92018-5100, USA
Hay House UK Ltd, The Sixth Floor, Watson House, 54 Baker Street, London W1U 7BU, UK
Hay House Australia Publishing Pty Ltd, 18/36 Ralph St., Alexandria NSW 2015, Australia

Email: contact@hayhouse.co.in
Website: www.hayhouse.co.in

First published by Hay House India, 2024
10 9 8 7 6 5 4 3 2 1

ISBN 978-81-97328-55-8
ISBN 978-81-97328-50-3 (Ebook)

Printed at Replika Press Pvt Ltd

MIX
Paper | Supporting responsible forestry
FSC www.fsc.org FSC™ C016779

Hay House is committed to a sustainable future for our business, our readers and our planet. This book is made from Forest Stewardship Council® certified paper.

To all the altruistic individuals who could have spent their time endlessly scrolling through screens but instead chose to take the initiative to make this world a better place for you, for me, and for all living beings.

Contents

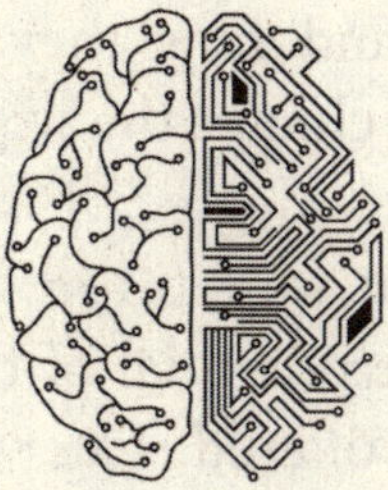

Preface

'The true test of civilisation is not the census, nor the size of cities, nor the crops, but the kind of man that the country turns out.'

—Ralph Waldo Emerson

In 1997, when I was enrolled in a computer science program at a highly reputable college in Kerala, I was frequently asked about the practical applications of computer science. The question 'What can you do with a computer?' was a common one, but over the years, the question has evolved to include inquiries about the capabilities of computers and if there is anything they cannot do. Back then, the attitudes and perceptions towards computers were very different than they are today. At that time, computers were seen as mere tools for data processing and not much else. But now, with the advancements in technology, we understand the immense power of computers and how they can be used to solve complex problems and change the world.

During my master's degree, I specialised in artificial intelligence, a field that was still in its infancy at that time. I was fascinated by the potential of this technology and the endless possibilities it offered. Later, I had the opportunity to teach artificial intelligence at the university where my students often asked the question 'What can be done with artificial intelligence?' But now, we have a clear understanding of the capabilities of AI and how it can be used in various fields, from healthcare and finance to transportation and manufacturing. It has surpassed our wildest imaginations and all expectations.

However, like any powerful tool, artificial intelligence also has its downsides. Just as drinking too much water can be dangerous, even something as beneficial as AI can have negative consequences if not used responsibly. The development and use of AI must be guided by ethical principles and a deep understanding of its potential impact on society. It is important to strike a balance between utilising the benefits of AI while also mitigating its negative consequences.

It was a fortunate coincidence that I had the opportunity to study the field of cyberpsychology abroad. My previous studies and work experience in the areas of computer science, psychology, and human resource management led me to this field. Subsequently, I had the opportunity to work in this field in various countries.

The field of information technology is one of the most revolutionary in human history and must be handled with care. A term called 'scientism' exists, which refers to an overconfidence in science and its methods, and in what is considered 'scientific'. On one hand, superstition thrives; on the other, the idea that science can never be wrong and is akin to a religion is gaining ground. It is important to note that it is a form of fanaticism to think that anything labelled as science can be blindly accepted. Many misguided actions, misunderstandings, and incorrect ways of life have been followed based on claims that were believed to be scientifically proven.

Working at a research institute of a prestigious university, I have come to understand that corporations often do not view research as a means to discover the truth. This is not the reason they fund research. Instead, it is solely an effort to achieve their desired outcome. Therefore, it is crucial to analyse even science in a scientific manner. Only mathematics is 100 per cent logical, while the rest falls within the realm of logic. Therefore, if something is labelled as scientifically proven, it does not mean it should be blindly accepted. In fact, there are hundreds of false studies like this in peer-reviewed journals. The important thing to realise is that Science is constantly evolving, and we must be vigilant in critically analysing and assessing new findings.

As someone who is highly attuned to technology, I believe that science should not be placed above humanity. With this belief, I have written this book with the intention of highlighting the issues that arise with technology and the belief that humanity can greatly benefit through the responsible use and application of technology. The products of science can be examined with a purely scientific perspective, but it is important to remember that they should also be evaluated in terms of their impact on humanity. As the saying goes, 'I will not love any philosophy that does not love humanity.'

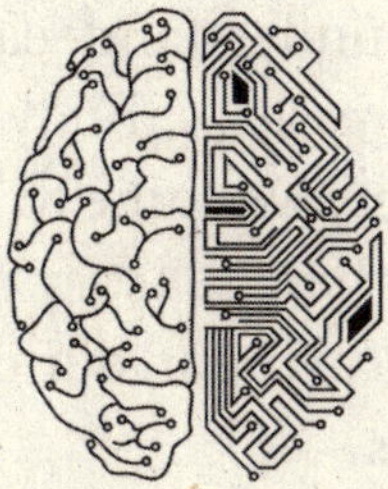

Chapter 1
HOW CYBERSPACE TRANSFORMS HUMAN BEHAVIOUR

TECHNOLOGY HAS ALWAYS PLAYED A SIGNIFICANT ROLE IN shaping human behaviour, and the internet and smartphones have been among the most powerful influences. Cyberspace, in particular, can transport us to a different world where our language, clothing, attitudes, personalities, desires, and emotions can all change drastically. For example, individuals who inhabit the cyber world may engage in actions that they would otherwise hesitate to perform in reality. In fact, each of us is undergoing a transformation without even realising it. Therefore, measuring one's cyber personality is not an easy task for psychologists.

The illusion that the cyber world is safer and has fewer consequences than the real world often drives people to engage in extreme behaviour. They perceive fewer risks in digital interactions compared to face-to-face contact. However, our instincts are honed and developed for the real world. Humans have evolved, survived, and built this civilisation as social beings. We understand each other through the exchange of facial expressions, body language, and the use of our senses. This is how we come to know our companions. In digital interactions, these sensory possibilities are limited, and without such physical input, our understanding of others can often be inaccurate.

When we use social media, our confidence tends to increase significantly since we don't have face-to-face interaction with others. The absence of physical presence eliminates our inhibitions and fear of judgement, creating a feeling of anonymity and invincibility. However, this false sense of security, along with the belief of being unobserved, results in the online disinhibition effect, a well-known phenomenon in cyberpsychology. This effect can lead to people engaging in more audacious behaviour, similar to the effects of drugs and alcohol. Additionally, the impact of cyberspace on individuals can be profound, resulting in behaviour that can differ from how they behave in real life. For example, people engage in dangerous activities online, such as being exposed to inappropriate content and engaging in illicit activities. This can cause feelings of shame, guilt, and even personality disorders. Thus, it is important to understand that the transition from the physical world to the virtual world can be rapid and drastic, emphasising the importance of being aware of the potential risks associated with engaging in online activities.

Growth of Unconventional Sexual Fantasy

The depiction of unconventional sexual fantasy is explored in the Hollywood film *Fifty Shades of Grey*, which has captured the imaginations of audiences worldwide. Based on a book of the same name, the story follows the relationship between

Christian Gray, a wealthy entrepreneur, and Anastasia Steele, a literature student, as they fall in love. However, the relationship is complicated by Gray's reservations about sex and his preference for BDSM, which stands for bondage, discipline/dominance, submission/sadism, and masochism. The book delves into two serious sexual disorders, namely sadism disorder and sexual masochism disorder, which are further explored in the film.

The important takeaway here is that the *Fifty Shades of Grey* book trilogy had a significant impact on the BDSM community and its popularity. In the years following the publication of the books, internet searches for BDSM porn videos increased by 67 per cent globally. The correlation between the rise in popularity of BDSM and the *Fifty Shades of Grey* trilogy is further highlighted by the increase in searches for terms such as 'sex slave' and 'master', which rose by approximately 79 per cent and 72 per cent, respectively. This increase in interest in BDSM has also been reflected in the growth of BDSM communities, such as Vancouver-based pansexual social networking site FetLife. The FetLife community has more than tripled in size, growing from a membership base of just a few hundred thousand to over 3.5 million members in just a few short years. The members of the FetLife community have been extremely active, sharing over 19 million photos and 1,72,000 videos, participating in 4.7 million discussions, and creating 1.7 million blog posts. These figures were recorded in 2015 and provide a snapshot of the growth and popularity of the BDSM community in the years following the publication of the *Fifty Shades of Grey* trilogy. And though previous attempts have been made to commercialise paraphilia (abnormal or atypical sexual cravings, fantasies, and behaviours), such as Madonna's best-selling coffee-table book, *Sex,* from 1992 and Luis Buñuel's classic 1967 film, *Belle de Jour,* which portrays a young woman engaging in fetishes, the widespread accessibility of media, particularly thanks to the internet, such sexual fantasies have proliferated significantly.

It's also important to recognise that the increased connectivity and the proliferation of online communities centred around various interests, including sexual ones, has introduced new complexities and potential dangers not prevalent in the pre-internet era. Hence, it's essential for individuals to be mindful of the potential risks involved and exercise discretion in their online engagements. In the next section, we will delve into this phenomenon in greater detail.

Cyber-socialisation

Cyber-socialisation is characterised by forming online connections that bring together people with similar interests. This is its greatest advantage—allowing individuals to connect with others from all over the world, gaining insight into different lifestyles and situations. It broadens their social perspectives and can foster understanding and empathy for strangers.

Additionally, the internet offers solace to those socially isolated due to distance or personality issues, providing a place to find meaningful relationships anytime, anywhere. For example, in cyberspace, individuals often partake in behaviours and activities online they wouldn't pursue in the real world, given the anonymity and absence of geographical constraints. As covered before, those with BDSM and other unconventional sexual interests previously faced difficulty finding partners or communities that shared their inclinations. However, the rise of the internet and social media has made it easier for people with varied interests to connect with like-minded individuals and normalise their behaviours. Platforms like Telegram and WhatsApp provide means to socialise, facilitate, and syndicate these interests.

Despite this advantage of forming online relationships and making friends, seamless internet access also has negative effects, as individuals have limited social information beyond the screen, making it difficult to rely on real-world instincts. And though some might argue online interactions are more appealing and safer than physical ones, numerous cases of catfishing and online stalking exist. Thus, it's crucial to recognise that online interactions carry their own risks.

To summarise, while the appeal of online communities lies in connecting with like-minded people sharing similar interests, exercising vigilance and caution when engaging in online relationships is vital to avoid inappropriate or dangerous behaviour.

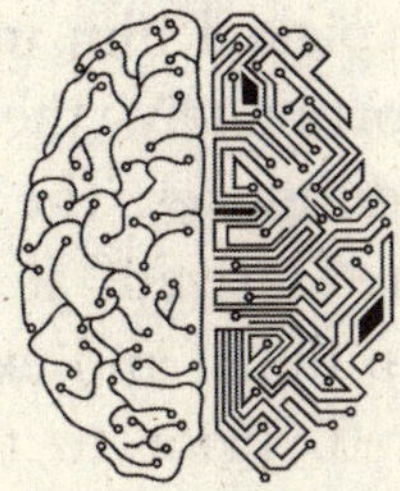

Chapter 2
Wired and Restless

Digital Age: Boosting Impulsive Tendencies

In Florida, USA, 22-year-old Alexandra Tobias called 911. She informed the operator that her three-month-old son, Dylan, had stopped breathing and needed resuscitation. Alexandra told the police that their pet dog had pushed the infant off the couch, causing him to hit his head on the floor.

Investigators and doctors were suspicious of Alexandra's story. They questioned her repeatedly until she finally broke down in tears and revealed the truth. As it turned out, Alexandra had recently lost her mother, and her boyfriend had also left her after getting her pregnant. Overwhelmed by loneliness, she turned to Facebook seeking solace.

On that fateful day, Alexandra had been playing an online game called *Farmville* on her computer when she heard the cries of her baby Dylan. She was angry that her game was being disrupted, and when the child didn't stop crying, she reluctantly picked him up and began swinging him in a circle. Unfortunately, the child's head hit her computer, causing head injuries. The child was pronounced dead by the time he arrived at the hospital. Tobias confessed everything in detail and expressed deep remorse for what had transpired. Prior to this incident, she had aspirations of attending college and pursuing a successful career in order to support her child. However, things did not turn out as she had hoped.

In 2010, the Facebook online game, *Farmville,* garnered a significant player base of 60 million active users. In this virtual game, players could assume the role of farmers, planting crops, raising livestock and poultry, and building their virtual farms. Facebook itself had warned that the game was highly addictive. Despite these warnings, many players, including Alexandra, became hooked on the game's immersive experience. While her virtual farm flourished, her real life suffered. Her impulsive behaviour and addiction to the game ultimately resulted in the tragic loss of her child and ruined her future.

Impulsive behaviour refers to sudden and unplanned actions, and it has been found to be a key factor in many clinical conditions, including attention deficit hyperactivity disorder, borderline personality disorder, the manic phase of bipolar disorder, alcohol and drug abuse, and pathological gambling. The important thing to note here is that technology can significantly increase impulsive behaviour, as seen in the case of Alexandra Tobias. Her impulsive actions resulted in a tragedy that carried severe consequences. She was found guilty of second-degree murder and received a maximum sentence of fifty years in a Florida prison. This outcome serves as an unfortunate reminder of the potentially devastating consequences of impulsive behaviour brought on by technology.

The truth is that we are all impulsive to some degree, but this tendency has been magnified in the digital age. Activities such as multiplayer gaming, checking emails, posting on social networks, and even online gambling have overwhelmed our senses, leading to impulsive behaviours that can have far-reaching consequences on our lives and well-being. In conclusion, while technology offers numerous benefits and conveniences, it also poses significant risks by amplifying impulsive behaviours. It is essential for individuals to recognise the impact of technology on their impulses and take proactive steps to manage and control their digital habits.

The Global Concern of Internet and Video Game Addiction

In South Korea, the issue of internet addiction is widely recognised, researched, diagnosed, and treated as a serious condition. According to studies, approximately 20 per cent of Korean teenagers are considered to be internet addicts, with many struggling to function in their daily lives due to the severity of their addiction. The situation in China is reported to be even more concerning, with 13.7 per cent of Chinese teenage internet users being classified as addicted. Video game addiction is noted to be the most prevalent form of internet addiction, with countries such as China, Taiwan, South Korea, and Thailand having the highest number of gaming addicts.

Video game addiction (VGA), also known as gaming disorder or internet gaming disorder, is commonly defined as the problematic and uncontrollable use of video games. It significantly affects normal functioning in all areas of a person's life. The prolonged use of internet video or mobile games has a significant impact on certain areas of the brain, including the reward system, impulse control, and sensory-motor coordination. Research has shown that playing video games can lead to changes in the volume of the ventral striatum, the brain region responsible for reward and pleasure. Furthermore, functional magnetic resonance imaging (fMRI) scans have revealed that playing video games can result in a release of dopamine, a neurotransmitter associated with pleasure, in the brain. This effect is similar to that seen in drug abuse and gambling. Moreover, gaming addiction poses a serious health risk, particularly among the younger generation. This disorder is often accompanied by mental health issues such as depression, anxiety, and ADHD, which can lead to life-threatening consequences. Moreover, prolonged gaming can also result in a range of health issues such as wrist pain, poor hygiene, and irregular eating habits, among others. Therefore, it is essential to seek help for compulsive gaming behaviour, as it can be fatal if left unchecked.

Chris Staniforth, a twenty-year-old man from Sheffield, England, had a clear passion in life: online gaming. He would spend countless hours playing one of the most popular online military science fiction shooters, *Halo.* His father David Staniforth fondly remembers the times when Chris would sit and play for hours on end. But one night, after a day of gaming, Chris awoke in the middle of the night with a strange pain in his chest. The following day, while out with a friend, the pain returned and eventually led to his death. Doctors later confirmed that the cause of death was a pulmonary embolism—a fat clot from his legs had dislodged and travelled to his lungs, blocking the arteries and resulting in his death. This medical condition is known as deep vein thrombosis (DVT). It is a serious condition caused by sitting in one place for too long, with the most common sufferers being gamers, long-haul air travellers, and immobile hospital patients. Tragically, this was also the case for NBC White House correspondent, David Bloom, who died in Iraq in 2003 after sitting in a tank for prolonged periods of time. The Centers for Disease Control and Prevention estimates that around 1,00,000 Americans every year are killed by DVT-related pulmonary embolism.

Marathon gaming stations are particularly popular in Asian countries such as India, Korea, and China. These places are proliferated by internet cafes which are open round the clock to encourage gamers to participate in marathon competitive sessions. Unfortunately, this has led to tragedy in some cases, such as the story of 18-year-old Chuang, who collapsed and died after playing *Diablo* for 40 hours without food or sleep. In Taiwan, the body of 23-year-old Chen Rong Yu was discovered in a gaming centre, his arms still extended to the keyboard and mouse. In South Korea, a multi-billion-dollar professional gaming industry has emerged with over 20,000 PC bangs where gamers can play a plethora of multiplayer computer games by paying in advance.

Perhaps one of the most poignant examples of the risks of marathon gaming is the story of the married unemployed couple who were addicted to the game *Prius Online.* Obsessed with the virtual reality game, they became neglectful of their own infant child, leading to the young one's premature death due to malnutrition. The incident was documented by HBO in the 2014 movie, *Love Child.* There also have been numerous reports in the media of disturbing game-related incidents, some of which are so frightening that they are hard to comprehend. For example, in 2010, a mother in Korea repeatedly asked her 22-year-old son to quit playing video games. Unfortunately, her constant harassment led to a tragic outcome: the son murdered her and left her body behind as he rushed back to the internet cafe to continue gaming.

China was among the first nations to recognise excessive internet use and gaming as a clinical condition. The issue of uncontrolled gaming is particularly severe in the country. To address this, the government has established numerous treatment centres to help cure internet addiction among teenagers. In South Korea, the situation is similar, with individuals sacrificing sleep, education, employment, and real-life relationships to play online games. This increasing number of addicted teenagers has become a concern for the government, leading to the implementation of the Shutdown law in 2011. This law prohibits individuals under the age of 16 from accessing the internet between midnight and 6:00 a.m. and individuals under 18 from playing online games during the same hours. Parents or guardians who permit such activity may also be held responsible for violating the law.

By 2015, there were 500 inpatient facilities in Korea specifically dedicated to helping individuals overcome gadget addiction. In addition, every school has implemented prevention programs to address the issue. In the same year, the Taiwanese government also took action by passing a law which imposed a fine of up to 50,000 Taiwan dollars ($1,595 US) on parents whose children were found to be using electronic devices for an excessive amount of time. However, in the United States, the danger posed by excessive gaming has yet to be fully recognised. There are ongoing discussions to classify eSports or gaming as an official college athletic sport but this idea has been criticised by experts such as Kimberly Young, who argue that promoting such a potentially harmful activity is irresponsible. Unfortunately, it seems that many in the United States, like in other parts of the world, believe that they are immune to the negative effects of gaming. Senator Josh Hawley from Missouri, United States, is proposing legislation to address addictive practices in social media. As a Republican, Hawley is making a significant accusation, claiming that social media companies have deliberately developed a business model that relies on addiction and psychological manipulation. The World Health Organisation (WHO) has acknowledged the existence of gaming disorder and has included it in the 11th revision of its International Classification of Diseases (ICD). However, the American Psychiatric Association (APA) has not yet officially recognised gaming disorder as a mental disorder, stating that there is insufficient evidence to include it in the 2013 Diagnostic and Statistical Manual of Mental Disorders (DSM). Nonetheless, they acknowledge the need for further study in this area

The Psychology of the Lottery

In the USA, the Powerball lottery attracts a large number of enthusiastic participants. The odds of winning are incredibly low at one in 300 million. This phenomenon can be explained by the principles of behavioural psychology, which states that random, intermittent rewards are more effective in motivating people than consistent rewards. The unpredictability of the rewards makes the activity more enticing and engaging, leading individuals to participate more willingly.

The famous study on pigeons supports the concept that intermittent rewards are more motivating than consistent rewards. The results showed that the pigeons were more likely to engage in a certain activity when they were randomly rewarded, as opposed to being rewarded every single time. This highlights the impact of variability in rewards on motivation and behaviour

Similarly, scratch-and-win tickets have been found to have a direct impact on the release of dopamine in the brain. Dopamine is a chemical messenger that helps regulate emotions and is associated with positive feelings. When dopamine is released, it creates a feeling of euphoria and can be highly addictive. This explains the strong appeal of scratch-and-win tickets, which can result in compulsive behaviour. Even if you don't win, the momentary thrill makes you feel happy and prompts you to keep scratching cards. Additionally, the resulting euphoria created by biochemicals puts you in a feedback loop, making you want to buy more lottery tickets. The same phenomenon occurs in gambling, as it too provides a rush of excitement and pleasure.

From Loans to Embezzlement: The Dark Side of OnlineGambling

Vineeth, a 29-year-old ISRO employee from Thiruvananthapuram, started playing online rummy during the Covid lockdown. He became too indulgent in the game, reportedly taking loans from several private banks to fund his play. Overwhelmed by debt, he tragically committed suicide.

People from all walks of life have lost money to online gambling, though little has been reported by the media. This addictive gambling prompted Bijulal, an accountant at the state treasury, to embezzle Rs 2.7 crore. A policeman from Ernakulam A. R. camp, in debt due to online rummy addiction, was arrested for stealing gold from a friend's house. The branch manager of Punjab National Bank's Kozhikode branch was found to have embezzled Rs 15 crore to fuel an online lottery habit.

According to India's Gambling Act, only 'games of chance' can be penalised. The government interprets this to mean games requiring skill are permissible. Due to this interpretation, the online gambling industry has boomed, with abundant apps, websites, ads featuring celebrities, and newspaper promotions. There is a need to regulate this industry with guidelines that protect people from falling into damaging addictions.

Compulsive Consumerism

In recent years, due to the convenience and widespread access to the digital marketplace, it has become increasingly easy to purchase items online without needing to own the funds upfront. This has resulted in many people buying items that they otherwise wouldn't have, or worse, cannot afford. In some cases, this habit has been identified by experts as a type of addiction.

Donald Black, a professor of psychiatry at the University of Iowa College of Medicine, attests to the fact that this type of consumerism is actively promoted by consumer culture and corporations. He posits that it's a form of compulsive-shopping disorder, closely related to the more widely known obsessive-compulsive disorder. This behaviour is largely indicative of American culture, where shopping for the latest goods is seen as a status symbol and a way of expressing pride in one's possessions.

Unfortunately, this addiction can have a severely detrimental effect on people's financial well-being, as they may be tempted to purchase items that they cannot afford, leading to a cycle of debt and anxiety. Beyond the financial strain, this compulsive behaviour can also affect mental health, causing feelings of guilt, shame, and depression. Addressing this issue requires a multifaceted approach, including increased public awareness, mental health support, and perhaps more stringent regulations on how consumer goods are marketed online. Without such measures, the ease of online shopping may continue to drive individuals into deeper financial and psychological distress.

The Restless Technology

In the late 1960s and early 1970s, psychologist Walter Mitchell from Stanford University conducted an experiment known as the Stanford Marshmallow Experiment. In the experiment, children were offered a choice between a small, immediate reward (such as a marshmallow, dessert, or chocolate) or two small rewards if they waited for 15 minutes. The children were left alone in the room to make their decision.

During the experiment, some children were able to wait 15 minutes to double their rewards, while others struggled. This study has been ongoing for decades, with researchers discovering that children who exhibit the ability to wait for better rewards tend to have higher entrance scores, higher educational attainment, better health, and overall better life outcomes. However, technology, particularly cell phones and the internet, undermines the concept of delayed gratification. People now expect immediate responses to messages they send and desire instant access to information and services. This shift towards immediate gratification can lead to impatience and frustration when things don't happen as quickly as expected. Additionally, the constant availability of technology encourages a culture of multitasking, which can reduce overall productivity and increase stress levels. This instant-access mindset can also diminish the ability to plan for the long term, as people become more focused on short-term rewards. Over time, this can erode important skills such as patience, perseverance, and the ability to delay gratification, which are crucial for personal and professional growth.

Internet Addiction and Gender Relations

Boys with ADHD or aggressive behaviour have an increased likelihood of becoming addicted to the internet, while girls diagnosed with depression or social phobia are more susceptible to developing an internet addiction. It is important to note that correlation does not equal causation; meaning that just because there is a correlation between these conditions and internet addiction, it doesn't mean that one causes the other.

Children diagnosed with ADHD may experience social isolation from their peers due to their physical impulsiveness and antisocial behaviour. As a result, they may find solace in computer games as a way to escape misunderstanding and lack of appreciation from their peers. These children often exhibit hyperactivity, restlessness, and difficulty focusing, making them susceptible to getting fully engrossed in games that provide an exciting and stimulating experience. Parents may find comfort in seeing their hyperactive child sit still while playing videos and consider it a positive outcome.

It is important to take into consideration whether game production companies are aware of the fact that they have some social responsibilities when they make games that are used by young people. We need to assess what is their moral responsibility towards the welfare of the public. Food manufacturers are required by law to list calorie content and ingredients on their packaging. There has been positive opposition from the community against fast food companies like McDonald's and soft drinks like Coca-Cola. Similarly, all of these game designs have an element of human exploitation, yet no government has set any standards to regulate its addiction. Thus, there is an urgent need for regulations and restrictions to be put in place to keep a check on these games and the companies producing them.

The Impact of Excessive Internet Use

Depression is a prevalent mental health issue that frequently co-occurs with anxiety disorders. Numerous studies in psychology and neuroscience have demonstrated that excessive internet use among adolescents can have negative effects on their social, behavioural, and health outcomes. Activities such as online chatting, visiting explicit websites, playing games, and online gambling are particularly associated with these detrimental effects. These behaviours can lead to decreased academic performance, disrupted daily routines, dysfunctional relationships, and even violent behaviour. Let's examine some of these impacts in more detail.

1. Academic Performance

Excessive internet use can harm academic performance. Adolescents who spend too much time online often neglect their studies, leading to lower grades, reduced participation in school activities, and a lack of motivation for academic achievement. Constant online engagement distracts them, impairs concentration, and leaves less time for homework and study.

2. Habits and Routines

Unregulated use of the internet use can disrupt daily routines. Staying up late for online activities results in insufficient and irregular sleep patterns, adversely affecting physical health. This disruption can cause fatigue, weakened immune systems, and other health issues.

3. Relationships

Excessive internet use can harm relationships. Spending too much time online reduces face-to-face interactions with family and friends, leading to communication breakdowns, feelings of isolation, and loneliness. The lack of real-world social interactions impedes the development of crucial social skills and emotional intelligence.

4. Behaviour

There is a correlation between excessive internet use and violent behaviour among teenagers. Engaging in inappropriate online activities, such as viewing explicit content and playing violent games, has been linked to heightened aggression. Exposure to violent content desensitises adolescents to violence, increasing the likelihood of real-life aggressive behaviour.

5. Mental Health

Compulsive internet usage can contribute to various mental health issues. Prolonged exposure to social media and online interactions can lead to feelings of inadequacy, anxiety, and depression. Cyberbullying, online harassment, and social comparison further erode self-esteem and mental well-being.

6. Development

Internet overindulgence can hinder adolescents' behavioural development. During a critical stage of identity formation, extensive online engagement can distort perceptions and promote maladaptive behaviours that may persist into adulthood.

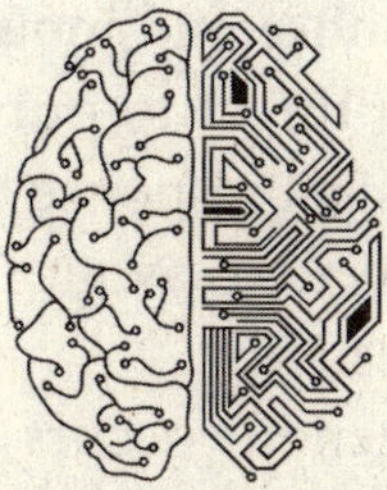

Chapter 3

The Dark Side of Screens

Mechanical Feeding

I recently attended a marriage function at a posh resort, which had a great ambience. Everyone was enjoying their food in silence until a young mother began playing loud cartoons on her mobile phone for her 3-year-old child. This disrupted the peaceful atmosphere and annoyed everyone in the room. While the mother automatically pushed food into her child's mouth, it seemed like she was unaware of the social harm being caused by her actions.

It is essential to understand that eating is not merely an insignificant mechanical process and instead involves all our senses. The surrounding sounds, colour, temperature, and smell of the food we eat can affect our enjoyment and digestion. Therefore, there are physical, social, and mental etiquettes to follow while eating. So, when food is forced into someone's mouth while they are engaged in another activity, like watching cartoons, the brain will resist it. Due to the close proximity of the nose and mouth, our brain perceives any external force as a threat to our lives. Due to this, our psychological and physical response to that food may not be optimal. Thus, it is crucial to savour the experience of eating and enjoy it to the fullest.

A similar phenomenon occurs during breastfeeding, often viewed as an automatic process that can be done while multitasking. However, is it appropriate to treat feeding one's child as a mere duty, without giving it the attention it deserves? Many busy mothers may lack time to lavish nursing babies with affection. But some politicians, like Brazilian Minister Manuela D'Ávila, Canadian Minister Karina Gould, New Zealand Prime Minister Jacinda Ardern, British MP Jo Swinson, Australian Senator Larissa Waters, Swedish MEP Jytte Guteland, and Carolina Bescanza in Spain, have brought babies to work and breastfed during parliamentary sessions. While this is commendable, it is disheartening to see mothers without such responsibilities preoccupied with phones or distractions while breastfeeding. Meanwhile, their babies gaze up in wonder as the mother feeds mechanically, without taking time to connect. How many millions of parents worldwide make this mistake of giving more attention to phones and other digital distractions than their babies during feedings or communication? This behaviour can harm the next generation, as studies have demonstrated.

In summary, while regulating screen time for child safety is important, we must also address the issue of its potential long-term effects on adults.

The Importance of Physical Affection in Baby Development

Giving your baby attention goes beyond just providing them

with food and changing their diapers. It is crucial to show physical affection by hugging, kissing, and engaging with them through talking, tickling, massaging, and playing. Physical contact is vital for a baby's development, and eye contact is especially important as it allows them to connect with you on an emotional level.

When you interact with your baby, they can perceive your emotions through your facial expressions. Showing them love, attention, and occasional affectionate teasing is critical for their mental and emotional growth. These interactions help build the foundation for the child's emotional bond with their parents and caregivers, which is crucial for their future relationships. And when a child forms a secure attachment with their parent through regular interactions, their emotional foundation for future relationships is more stable. A secure attachment pattern helps the child interact with others easily, leading to greater confidence and self-respect. Moreover, an individual's attachment style can impact how they form friendships, choose a life partner, and handle the end of relationships.

In the 1930s, American psychologist Harry F. Harlow conducted studies on mother-infant relationships using rhesus monkey infants as subjects. His research mainly focused on the impact of maternal separation on children. Professor Harlow's observations led him to realise that monkeys raised in nurseries without their mothers exhibited different behaviour compared to those raised with their mothers. These orphaned monkeys appeared dazed and confused, exhibiting unusual behaviours. Additionally, he noticed that these baby monkeys were highly attached to the soft blankets in their cages. Removing these blankets to be cleaned caused distress, causing them to curl up and suck their thumbs. This led Harlow to believe that the physical closeness and presence of mothers and babies were much more crucial than previously believed. Surprisingly, during this time, caregivers in orphanages, childcare institutions, and hospitals were prohibited from having physical contact with infants, as such intimacy was considered unnecessary and unhealthy.

Harlow conducted another experiment where he presented two artificial mother monkeys in front of orphaned baby monkeys. One of the mother monkeys was made of wireframes and had a milk bottle to feed the baby, while the other was made of soft velvet fabric but had no milk bottle. To Harlow's surprise, all of the baby monkeys preferred the mother made of soft velvet fabric, even though it had no milk. They spent their days hugging and cuddling it, only approaching the mother with the milk bottle when they were hungry. This experiment showed that physical contact and comfort were just as crucial as food for infant monkeys' well-being. This experiment also clearly demonstrated that love and bonding with infants is not limited to feeding and that physical intimacy is a critical psychological resource that strengthens infants emotionally. These findings had a significant impact on the understanding of the importance of physical contact and attachment in child development, leading to changes in how caregivers interact with infants in institutions such as orphanages and hospitals.

In a new experiment conducted by Harlow, the caged monkeys were exposed to loud noises and other stimuli meant to frighten them. When this happened, the baby monkeys sought comfort from their soft cloth mother. They would cling to the velvet cloth and sit quietly until they felt better.

The human brain is often described as 'plastic,' meaning that it can change physically, functionally, and chemically over time. While the comforting presence of a terry-cloth mother was beneficial for the baby monkeys in Harlow's experiments, human babies require more than just tactile comfort. Research has shown that a lack of emotional and social care during certain critical periods of childhood can have devastating consequences. Healthy attachment or connectivity patterns have been shown to be important for a child's intellectual growth and development.

Overall, the research conducted by Harlow and others emphasises the importance of physical and emotional closeness between parents and infants. Babies require more than just food and basic necessities; they need hugs, kisses, and physical contact to feel secure and develop emotionally. Neglecting these needs can have long-lasting consequences on a child's well-being and future relationships.

The Impact of Technology on Parent-Child Bond

As covered in the previous section, emotional bonding and engagement between a mother and her baby play a significant role in a child's healthy development. A crucial aspect of this bond is mutual eye contact, which is an evolutionary trait that helps babies get the attention they need from their caregivers. The cute and cuddly appearance of babies prompts adults to nurture and protect them, a trait that is common across species and essential for the survival of the young.

It is also important to note that this bonding and connectivity may not develop properly in environments where children experience neglect or abuse, such as large orphanages and daycare centres. This deficit can even impede the formation of neural pathways necessary for learning and cognitive development. There have been reported cases of children raised in isolation or in the wild, which have provided valuable insights into the critical role of early experiences and caregiver interactions in shaping a child's development. At least nine such cases have been documented over the past century. And while the effects of such isolation vary depending on the age at which human contact was removed and the disorders developed, many of these children exhibited unhealthy behaviours, underscoring the importance of human interaction in early childhood development.

The increasing use of electronic gadgets and screen time among parents often diverts attention away from their babies. A 2014 study in paediatrics observed many mothers using mobile phones while eating with their infants at fast food restaurants. Such distractions can override basic nurturing instincts, causing parents to neglect their babies' need for attention and interaction. Moreover, in many households, older siblings may prioritise screen time over engaging with their younger siblings, potentially leading to neglect and harm.

As mentioned, a strong emotional bond and engagement between a mother and her baby are crucial for the child's healthy development. Neglect, abuse, and excessive use of electronic devices can have devastating consequences on a child's cognitive and emotional well-being. While Western governments regulate certain aspects of childcare, such as car seat designs and product warnings, the growing lack of human interaction is a less obvious but significant concern. Reduced face-to-face communication may diminish people's ability to form deep connections, leading to fewer friendships, relationships, and mutual trust. This lack of interaction could impact future generations, making them less loving, caring, and interactive.

To summarise, humans are inherently social beings, and reciprocity is a basic survival instinct. However, with the rise of technology and social media, people are becoming increasingly isolated and less likely to interact in person. This lack of face-to-face interaction may even alter the course of human civilisation by changing how we communicate and form relationships.

The Rise of Screen Time and Its Implications

In the future, it may become necessary to include a warning on mobile phones and other popular gadgets regarding their potential impact. Excessive screen time can have negative effects on a child's pre-academic skills, including empathy, social skills, and problem-solving abilities. These skills are better developed through unstructured and creative play, interacting with real people, pets, toys, and objects. There is also concern about the potential risks of radiation exposure and the impact of the flickering light from screens on a baby's still-developing eyes. However, companies that produce mobile apps, video games, and other screen-based entertainment may not be willing to expose the dangers of excessive screen time due to profit and greed. Therefore, it is important to recognise the potential risks associated with excessive screen time in young children and to prioritise real-world interactions and playtime.

Numerous studies have been conducted on screen time and its implications, with the following points supported and verified by research:

- Until around age two, babies do not comprehend what they see on screens, meaning screens do not improve their knowledge, understanding, or cognitive abilities.
- When screens are in use, babies lose their inclination to independently play and explore their surroundings.
- The presence of screens leads parents to communicate less with their children, hindering the child's language acquisition.
- More screen time can diminish social interaction and the ability to interpret emotions from facial expressions.

Thus, we can see that while there is currently no evidence showing these electronic devices are harmful in the short term, they do deprive children of opportunities to engage in important real-life activities that contribute to mental and physical development. Research also suggests that children learn far more effectively from real-life experiences than from videos or screens, a phenomenon known as the video deficit effect. Additionally, studies show that exposure to constant background noise from television can hinder language development in young children, making direct communication with parents or caregivers a more effective means of language acquisition.

To conclude, in countries like India where the negative effects of screen time are not well-known, there is an urgent need to create better awareness and guidance, especially for parents, on the potential negative effects of technology.

When Should Children Begin Using Screens?

There are varying opinions and discussions regarding the impact of technology on children's health and development.

Some of these discussions are driven by the profit motives of companies invested in technology, while others are driven by conservative views, such as those expressed by paediatric occupational therapist Chris Rowan, who recommends limiting television and video game use for children.

As mentioned earlier, one concern about excessive screen time is that it may limit children's exposure to real-world experiences that are crucial for their mental and physical development. For example, a viral YouTube video shows a 1-year-old girl who struggles to understand the concept of turning pages in a print magazine because she is used to interacting with touchscreens. This suggests that children who spend too much time on screens may lag behind in the physical world and struggle to adapt to real-world experiences.

Another concern is that excessive screen time can disrupt children's sleep patterns. Paediatric sleep experts recommend avoiding stimulating activities before bedtime, including screen use. Screen light can disrupt circadian rhythms, leading to insomnia and other sleep disturbances. Furthermore, research suggests that excessive screen time may increase the risk of attention deficit disorders and other mental health issues in children. Studies have found a correlation between television and video game use and the development of ADHD, cognitive delays, learning disabilities, emotional suppression, and lack of self-regulation.

Overall, while technology can be useful and educational for children, it is important to set reasonable limits on screen time and prioritise real-world experiences for their mental and physical development. Encouraging activities such as outdoor play, reading physical books, and engaging in face-to-face social interactions can help balance their use of technology. By fostering a healthy relationship with digital devices, we can ensure that children develop critical life skills and maintain a well-rounded approach to learning and growth. Additionally, parents and educators should model balanced technology use to reinforce these habits and create a supportive environment for children.

The Limits of Social Connections

Stanford University anthropologist Professor Robin Dunbar explains that all intelligently developed mammals, including humans and apes, share the common feature of large brains, which are necessary to navigate socially complex environments. In fact, Prof. Dunbar suggests that an animal's group size can be predicted by the size of its neocortex, especially the frontal lobe. This is reflected in humans, who live in large groups and possess large brains. But the fact of the matter is that despite having the ability to make friends on social media platforms, such as Facebook, many people are limited in their capacity to maintain meaningful friendships. Prof. Dunbar conducted studies which found that individuals can only maintain meaningful relationships with a maximum of 150 people. When the number of relationships exceeds this number, individuals start to worry about their relationships 42 per cent of the time.

To illustrate this concept, Prof. Dunbar uses the analogy of a bowl filled with water. Just like adding more water to the bowl will result in wasted water, adding more people to your friendship circle will result in less meaningful relationships. This phenomenon is not due to limitations in the brain but rather due to evolutionary factors, such as limited energy, mental energy, and time. Therefore, having a large number of social media contacts does not necessarily translate to having real friends. It is important to understand that social media friends do not truly know you or care about you and that maintaining meaningful relationships requires time and effort.

In conclusion, while social media expands our ability to connect with others, it does not equate to genuine friendship. Prof. Dunbar's research highlights that meaningful relationships are limited by our cognitive and emotional capacities. Thus, investing time and effort into a smaller circle of true friends is essential for deeper, more fulfilling connections.

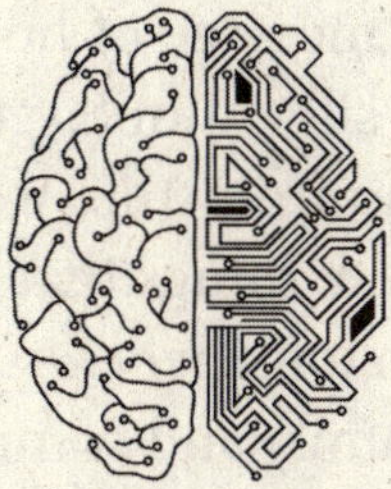

Chapter 4

Cyberbullying and Other Online Threats

Once upon a time, there was a vivacious and beautiful 12-year-old girl named Sarah Lynn Butler. She lived in Williford, a small town in Arkansas, USA, where she studied at the local school. One day, to her great excitement, she was chosen as the beauty queen of her school. Her mother described her as a child who was always happy and surrounded by many friends. However, her happiness was short-lived as she soon began receiving despicable messages on her MySpace account. These messages, calling her a prostitute and containing vulgar content, were a shock to the young girl who was just starting to blossom. Her mother soon discovered what was happening on her daughter's page and tried to help by blocking her friend's list.

But it was too late, the damage had already been done. One fateful afternoon, Sarah was home alone and logged into her MySpace account. It was there that she wrote her final post—a heartbreaking message of hopelessness and despair. She wrote, 'I'm just a silly, dumb, good-for-nothing girl. I know that if I am gone from this world, nobody will miss me. But I can't bear these things that other people say about me.' Tragically, she then took her own life by hanging, leaving behind her shattered family and community in disbelief.

The tragedy of Sarah's death serves as a cautionary tale of the dangers of cyberbullying. It is a reminder that the words we write and say online can have real and devastating consequences. We must be vigilant in protecting our young people from the cruel and harmful effects of cyberbullying. We must work together to create a kinder and safer world both online and offline. For Sarah Lynn Butler, it is too late, but we can honour her memory by being part of the solution to this prevalent issue.

The Growing Crisis of Cyberbullying

The rise of cyberbullying has become a major concern globally, with its devastating effects on children leading to an alarming increase in mental health issues such as anxiety and depression, physical harm, and even suicides. The impact of this form of bullying is so severe that it has become a common occurrence, leading to a growing sense of helplessness amongst parents and educators alike. In a poll conducted across twenty-four countries, it was found that 12 per cent of parents reported their child had experienced some form of cyberbullying. The nature of the attacks is often persistent and severe, with repeated critical remarks and teasing leaving young people feeling mentally and emotionally exhausted.

As social media has become an integral part of daily life, the number of instances of cyberbullying has grown exponentially. In the United States alone, an American survey found that over a million children experienced humiliation, bullying, or other forms of cybercrime on Facebook last year. Furthermore, the issue is not limited to just one social media platform but has become pervasive across all digital platforms.

Another important point to note here is that the impact of cyberbullying is not just limited to children but also affects adults. It is essential to raise awareness about this issue and provide support to those affected by it. We must work towards creating a safe and inclusive environment on all online platforms to prevent further harm caused by cyberbullying. It is crucial to empower individuals, especially young people, to speak out against cyberbullying and provide them with the necessary tools and resources to report and seek help. Only then can we hope to eradicate the issue of cyberbullying and create a safer and more inclusive world for everyone.

What Is Cyberbullying?

The US National Crime Prevention Council defines cyberbullying as 'the act of using the internet, cell phones, or other devices to send or post pictures or messages intended to hurt, humiliate, or defame another person.' In simple terms, bullying a person using the internet, cell phone, or other digital devices can be called cyberbullying. Cyberbullying includes sending harassing text messages to others, posting harmful information about a person, or making hateful comments. These comments can range from body-shaming and spreading false rumours to making threats and engaging in other forms of online harassment. Let's examine the various forms of cyberbullying.

- **Flaming:** Using hurtful language against a person in e-mails, text messages, or chat rooms.
- **Harassment:** Sending hurtful, hateful, and threatening messages.
- **Cyberstalking:** Following a person online and sending e-mails or messages to harass or threaten them.
- **Banning:** Deliberately banning a person from a group and posting hateful comments/messages about them.
- **Impersonation:** Publicly sharing true or false information about a person using a false identity to damage their reputation.
- **Trolling:** Deliberately hurting a person by posting insulting or inflammatory comments.
- **Fragging:** Using a person's social networking accounts to post inappropriate content that damages their reputation.

The Impact of Cyberbullying on Children

Cyberbullying can significantly affect a child, leading to various adverse effects such as:

- Low self-esteem.
- Tendency to spend time alone away from others.
- Reluctance to allow parents or family members to use their mobile phones or computers.
- Sudden weight loss or change in appearance.
- Changes in eating and sleeping patterns.
- Feeling insecure and humiliated.
- Coming up with excuses to stay away from school.

- Signs of skin injury indicating self-harm; trying to hide the wounds by wearing full-body clothing.
- Change in personality with increased anger, depression, and anxiety.
- Declining performance in academics, sports, and extracurricular activities.

The Escalating Cruelty of Cyberbullying

In the world of cyberbullying, cruelty has become a competitive sport. It begins with sharp, hurtful Facebook posts and soon escalates to sadistic behaviour. Celebrities are often the easy target of these kinds of vicious activities. Monica Lewinsky, one of the earliest social media victims, took a decade to recover from the ordeal. Even the daughter of the late actor Robin Williams, Zelda Williams, deleted her Twitter account after facing unimaginable abuse on the platform. These examples demonstrate that even adults find it challenging to cope with cyberbullying, highlighting how volatile and unsafe the online environment can be for children.

Consider a scenario where your two closest friends turned against you in real life. Imagine how much mental and emotional strain it would cause. Now, imagine if not just two, but thousands of people were opposing you. The pressure and stress would be overwhelming and could lead to depression and anxiety.

The important point to recognise here is that children and even adults may lack the psycho-social skills to handle online bullying. Our brain perceives any opposition as a threat to survival. This hypersensitivity to criticism can be particularly challenging for children to manage, as they may not have developed the emotional resilience to cope with the negativity of online interactions.

To summarise, the pervasive nature of cyberbullying highlights the urgent need for stronger protections and support systems, especially for children. The psychological toll it takes on victims, both young and old, underscores the importance of fostering emotional resilience and digital literacy. By addressing these issues, we can work towards creating a safer and more supportive online environment for everyone.

Understanding the Risks: Violence, Pornography, and Child Vulnerability

According to a survey of 4,000 adult men, 30 per cent admitted to viewing pornography on a daily basis. While older individuals may possess the self-control and knowledge required to resist the temptation to watch porn, the same cannot be said for children under the age of twelve. Their lack of maturity and understanding of such content makes them more vulnerable to its negative effects.

One of the most disturbing trends in the online world is the rise of 'sex tourism.' This abhorrent practice involves men from wealthy nations paying money to watch children perform sexual acts live via webcams in impoverished countries. These children, who are often forced or coerced into such situations, are subject to unimaginable trauma and abuse. Meanwhile, their clients sit in front of their computer screens and watch these innocent victims suffer. Additionally, internet gaming platforms and forums have become common places where predators target children, using webcams and microphones to communicate. Children can make mistakes by freely chatting and inadvertently revealing information, leaving them vulnerable to being taken advantage of.

Apart from safeguarding children against online predators, it is also crucial to protect them from inappropriate content online. Children described many things they saw on video-sharing websites, such as YouTube, as disturbing. They admitted that violent or sexual images, as well as other inappropriate content, bothered them. While most websites monitor their content, including YouTube, videos of violence and mature content are still available and easily accessible. Videos with inappropriate content often have thousands of views before they come to the attention of authorities. A tragic incident took place in Britain in 1993 that involved two 10-year-old boys who kidnapped and tortured a 2-year-old boy named Jamie to death. The boys had watched violent movies, including *Child's Play 3*, and were actively searching for a victim to imitate the atrocities they saw on the screen.

In the past, parents used to worry about their children's exposure to obscene magazines but that cannot compare to the problem we face today. Thousands of websites with billions of images and videos are easily accessible and cost nothing. The internet has made it easier than ever for predators to target vulnerable children, and the impact of their actions can be catastrophic. Hence, it is important to recognise that this behaviour is not only morally reprehensible but also illegal in many countries. Efforts must be made to crack down on this heinous practice and protect the innocent children who are exploited in this way. Parents must also be vigilant about their children's online activities and take steps to ensure their safety and well-being in the digital world.

The Bystander Effect

In 1964, a young woman named Catherine Genovese was murdered in New York City. Following that infamous murder, social psychologists Bib Latane and John Darley introduced the concept of the bystander effect. As per the report, many people saw an assailant chasing Catherine Genovese in the morning. He attacked her and then quickly left, but after the initial assault, Catherine was still alive. Unfortunately, the assailant returned and fatally stabbed her. Genovese repeatedly called for help and made distressed cries. A dozen people in a nearby apartment building later admitted to hearing her loud pleas for help but none of them called the police. The attack began around 3:20 a.m., but it wasn't until about half an hour later that someone finally called 911. The police arrived within two minutes, but by then, her life had ended.

In another case, a group of young men were harassing around sixty women in New York City's busy Central Park. Thousands of people must have witnessed it, yet not a single person tried calling the police. The villain here too was the bystander effect. Everyone likely assumed with so many people present, someone else would have called the authorities. Such incidents occur daily, with people remaining silent, hoping others will respond instead. Nowadays, bystanders even capture footage on their phones and share it on WhatsApp groups. This phenomenon is not limited to violent crimes but is also observed in accidents, where people assume others will help the victim, like hesitating to take an injured person to the hospital. Conversely, a lone victim is more likely to receive help if they are noticed.

To combat the bystander effect, educating people about its negative impacts and encouraging intervention is crucial, especially when someone needs help. Schools should conduct bystander effect workshops, urging people to speak up. Parents must teach children the importance of helping others and not being passive bystanders. By fostering compassion and empathy, we can prevent the bystander effect.

Dr Mary Aiken, an Irish cyberpsychology pioneer, suggests using the bystander effect to raise cyberbullying awareness among schoolchildren. In cyberbullying situations, many likely witness it but hesitate to intervene. Dr Aiken stresses never being a bystander to cyber-lynching. If one person intervenes, it can create a bandwagon effect encouraging others to join. As the number opposing the bully grows, even if just 10 out of 100, it provides great comfort to the victim.

Anti-Cyberbullying Laws

Intolerance in social media is becoming an accepted reality. No price or status in society changes this. A report by the Pew Research Center's Internet and American Life Project says that people being mean and cruel to others on social network sites has become increasingly common. Hence, it is important to establish and enact appropriate rules and laws that can aid in safeguarding people from various forms of online cyberbullying.

In India, though there are no specific laws to control cyberbullying, Section 66A of the Information Technology Act is useful for us. Harassing, offensive, and insulting communication through digital media and information communication technology is punishable under this Act.

Here are some additional rules that can be implemented to combat cyberbullying:

- Publication or transmission of obscene material—Section 67
- Publication or transmission of sexually suggestive material in electronic form—Section 67A
- Word, gesture, or act intended to insult the modesty of a woman—Section 509
- Sending defamatory messages by e-mail—Section 499 I.P.C.
- Printing of material defamatory or intended for blackmail—Section 292A
- Constantly digitally stalking and contacting a person, or attempting to contact a woman—Section 354D
- Making sexually coloured remarks—Section 354A
- Breach of privacy—Section 66 e
- Intimidation by anonymous communication—Section 507

A disheartening fact is that although laws exist to punish cyberbullying, very few victims and their families report such incidents. The majority prefer to remain silent, hoping the situation will resolve itself and improve on its own. Therefore, in order to bring about a change in people's mindset, there are some key points that policymakers should consider. For example, policymakers should adopt child-friendly policies that explain why cyberbullying is dangerous to children and society. There is also a need for a broad discussion on these in consultation with cybercrime experts, lawyers, academics, child rights activists, and educationists. Even countries with strict laws and regulations, such as the USA, Canada, and the UK, are struggling to control cyberbullying. However, unlike India, people in these countries consider fighting cyberbullying to be an imperative. Especially if the victims are school-going children. In such countries, schools have rules to deal with cyberbullying.

In short, parents should know that cyberbullying is not something that only affects children of a certain age. Parents should work with their children and ensure that they are well-informed about cyberbullying. This will help children to deal with cyberbullying if they face it.

Sweetie: Exposing Online Predators and Catalysing Legal Action

Let me tell you the story of a unique and powerful tool created to combat online child exploitation—Sweetie, the chatbot. Sweetie was an interactive 3D computer model designed to look and act like a 10-year-old Filipino girl. She was created by the advertising agency Lemz for Terre des Hommes, an international children's rights organisation based in the Netherlands.

One day, the Terre des Hommes team became aware of the growing problem of webcam sex tourism where men in wealthy countries pay children in impoverished nations to perform sexual acts via webcam. They knew undercover tactics were needed to catch these predators, and so Sweetie was born.

Within the first two and a half months of interacting online, Sweetie attracted nearly a thousand men from 71 different countries. Looking into her webcam, she would pleasantly say, 'Hello, my name is Sweetie,' and offer webcam sex for money. But Sweetie wasn't a real girl; she was software designed to capture the identities of child predators and provide them to law enforcement. Terre des Hommes estimated that 7,50,000 men worldwide were searching online for child sex at any given time.

As soon as Sweetie went live, Hans Guyt, Terre des Hommes' Special Projects Director, said people rushed there 'like an avalanche.' Sweetie gathered information like IP addresses and email addresses of those who contacted her. Using this data, Terre des Hommes identified over a thousand men willing to pay Sweetie for inappropriate activities and passed this information to law enforcement agencies globally, leading to the arrests of many perpetrators. Sweetie proved a powerful tool against online child exploitation, and her creators hope her legacy inspires similar efforts going forward.

How to Prevent Cyberbullying?

One of the most effective measures to prevent cyberbullying is by educating children about its harmful impacts. Given that many kids today use online platforms such as WhatsApp and Instagram, it is essential to make them understand the dangers associated with these platforms. To this end, schools can play a significant role by organising workshops on cyberbullying and sensitising children about its consequences.

In addition to schools, parents also need to take responsibility and educate their children about online safety. They should understand that electronic communication devices should not be treated as mere toys but rather as powerful tools that require proper handling. Parents should engage in frequent conversations with their children, monitor their online activities, and teach them about the importance of not sharing personal information with strangers. It is also crucial for parents to explain the serious implications of cyberbullying and observe any changes in their child's behaviour or attitude that may signal the occurrence of such incidents. By taking these proactive steps, both schools and parents can work together to prevent cyberbullying and create a safer online environment for children.

Empowering Parents: Strategies to Address Cyberbullying

If parents suspect a child has been subjected to cyberbullying, the matter should be reported to the relevant authorities. Here's what parents need to do:

- Identify and block the cyberbully's phone number and messages.
- Save all chats, posts, and emails sent by the perpetrator.
- Report the bully's phone number/account details to mobile service providers and social media platforms, which have reporting facilities.
- If bullying continues, register a complaint with the local police cybercrime cell.

A new McAfee Corporation study reveals Indian children have the highest online risk exposure, as parents provide them mobile phones at a very young age. The report titled 'Parents, Tweens, and Adolescents' Lives Behind the Screens' explains how the most vulnerable children are left unprotected in cyberspace.

In India, 83 per cent of children aged 10-14 use smartphones, 7 per cent higher than the 76 per cent international average. There's a significant gap between parents' and children's understanding of online safety, increasing risks for Indian children. 22 per cent have experienced cyberbullying, 5 per cent higher than the 17 per cent global average, yet Indian parents seem less concerned. While 90 per cent of global parents feel they must protect their children online, this awareness is slightly lower in India at 47 per cent, which is 10 per cent below the 57 per cent global average regarding cyberbullying and social media abuse concerns.

McAfee aims to educate parents on protecting against online risks like cyberbullying, identity theft, and financial information leaks. 33 per cent of Indian households report attempted account theft, which is 5 per cent above the global average. Indian families also report higher rates of financial disclosures than worldwide—21 per cent of parents (9 per cent above average) and 10 per cent of children (13 per cent above average).

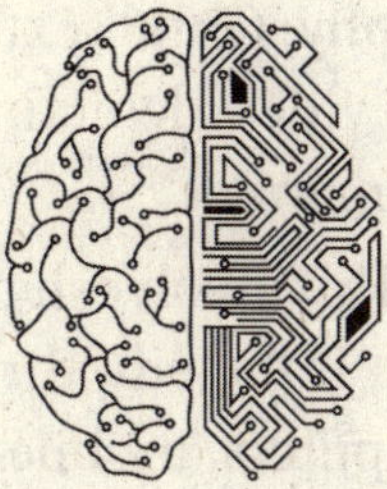

Chapter 5
The World of Cybercrime

Cybercrime can be defined as 'any illegal act involving the use of computers, cell phones, or computer networks to commit or facilitate a crime.' They are becoming increasingly common, and the consequences of these digital attacks can be devastating, causing serious damage. And as our world moves towards greater digitisation, the frequency and impact of cybercrimes are going to rise significantly.

Most cybercrimes fall under two main categories:

1. Criminal activity targeting computers.
2. Criminal activity using computers.

Various Types of Cybercrimes

Cybercrimes encompass both financial and non-monetary offences, impacting individuals, computers, and governments alike. Here are the main types of cybercrimes:

1. **Child Pornography:** Child sexual abuse material refers to any image or video depicting a child in a sexually explicit or nude manner.
2. **Cyberbullying:** This involves harassment, intimidation, or humiliation inflicted through communication devices like computers, mobile phones, laptops, or the internet.
3. **Cyberstalking:** A form of relentless stalking where a person persistently pursues another through electronic media.
4. **Cyber Grooming:** The act of establishing an online relationship with someone and coercing them into performing sexual acts.
5. **Online Job Fraud:** The fraudulent practice of extorting money from job seekers by making false promises of better jobs, higher wages, foreign employment opportunities, etc., taking advantage of the digital landscape.
6. **Online Sextortion:** Threatening to publish someone's personal information, pictures, or nude content online unless they provide money or other favours.
7. **Phishing:** A common tactic of stealing customer IDs, OTPs, and credit/debit card details by sending credible-seeming emails that trick recipients into clicking links which download information-stealing software.
8. **Vishing:** A cybercrime utilising phone calls, often from impersonators claiming authority like government, tax, police, or bank agents, to compel victims into revealing personal information through threats or pressure.

9. **Smishing:** Similar to phishing emails, this involves fake text messages aimed at stealing people's confidential personal or corporate data by prompting them to click malicious links masquerading as legitimate requests.
10. **Sexting:** The illegal sharing of sexually suggestive images and videos over the internet or electronic devices like smartphones.
11. **SIM Swap Scam:** In this scam, cybercriminals obtain a duplicate SIM card of a victim by exploiting weaknesses in two-factor authentication after gathering personal data like email, name, and phone number through phishing, enabling account access.
12. **Credit Card and Debit Card Fraud:** This includes unauthorised use of someone else's credit or debit card information to purchase goods or services, potentially maxing out the withdrawal limit.
13. **Identity Theft:** This involves fraudulently or dishonestly using someone else's electronic signature, password, or other unique identification feature, such as creating fake social media accounts or emails using another person's identity.
14. **Spamming:** This refers to receiving unsolicited commercial messages through email or SMS, often persuading recipients to buy products or services and potentially requesting bank account or credit card details.
15. **Ransomware:** This is a type of malicious software that prevents access to computer files, systems, or networks, with attackers blocking the entire system

and demanding a ransom to unlock it, potentially leading to the loss of critical information and data.

16. **Viruses, Worms, and Trojans:** These are computer programs that can damage, modify, or copy files/data, with viruses and Trojans potentially granting hackers system access and leading to theft of confidential and personal information.
17. **Data Breach:** This occurs when sensitive information is accessed without permission.
18. **Denial of Service:** An attack that renders a computer or network service unavailable for use, such as hackers sending more requests than a website can handle, preventing actual users from accessing it. A distributed denial of service (DDoS) attack involves traffic from multiple sources.
19. **Website Defacement:** This involves changing a website's appearance or disabling it, with attackers potentially posting obscene, hateful, or offensive content.
20. **Cyber-squatting:** An act of registering, misappropriating, or using a domain name with the intention of profiting from someone else's trademark.
21. **Pharming:** A cyberattack aimed at redirecting website traffic to another fake website, creating a convincing replica to deceive users.
22. **Cryptojacking:** This involves the unauthorised use of powerful processing systems for mining cryptocurrencies.
23. **Online Drug Trafficking:** This relates to the crime of selling, transporting, or illegally importing narcotic

drugs or controlled substances through electronic means.

24. **Espionage:** The act of obtaining data and information without the permission and knowledge of the owner.

Hacktivism

Hacktivism, a new form of activism emerging in the cyber realm, is a fusion of traditional activism and hacking. This decentralised operation is not carried out by any official organisation; rather, it involves individuals opposing governments, corporations, political organizations, and particular leadership by targeting entities that work against their beliefs and principles.

Hacktivist members do not operate as a cohesive group but as individuals who unite for a common cause. When a particular event prompts a response, they converge online, often comprising individuals with diverse ideas who temporarily set aside their backgrounds to collectively challenge perceived injustices. The term 'hacktivist' was coined in 1996 by a computer hacker nicknamed Omega, a long-time member of the notorious hacking group, Cult of the Dead Cow.

Hacktivists are typically motivated by ideological ideals, such as altruism, benevolence, social justice, freedom of speech, and democracy. Their objective is to disrupt online services and draw the attention of governments and people to a political or social cause. For instance, hacktivists may post a message on the homepage of a website to convey their message, which will be the first thing visitors see. And though hackers and hacktivists often use similar tools and techniques to achieve their goals, hackers typically don't advocate for social causes. Nevertheless, hacktivist activities are often considered illegal.

Hacktivists have been around for years, but the world did not really know about them until 2010 when Bradley Manning, one of the lowest-ranking personnel in the US Army, stole thousands of classified documents, videos, and diplomatic cables and gave them to Julian Assange, a publisher and an activist. Assange then published this information on the WikiLeaks website, and the world came to know about the many wrongdoings of the American government. After this event, following instructions and pressure from the US government, Mastercard and Bank of America cancelled all accounts associated with WikiLeaks in any way. This move angered WikiLeaks, prompting the notorious hacktivist group Anonymous to launch Operation Payback in response. They initiated cyberattacks, including denial of service attacks, against the companies that had cancelled WikiLeaks' accounts, resulting in losses amounting to billions of dollars for those companies at that time. The media coverage of the WikiLeaks leak, the subsequent DDoS attacks, and the social media response to it helped Anonymous and other hacktivists bring the concept of hacktivism into public consciousness.

Today, their popularity has become widespread, and they have even started recruitment efforts for hackers. Moreover, with the rise in internet connectivity, hacktivists have been able to create an army of cyber attackers across the globe. The notion of anonymity and lack of fear of repercussions have emboldened many to engage in hacktivism. As groups like Anonymous grew in prominence and received increased media coverage, hacktivist attacks have proliferated.

Various Types of Hacktivism

Hacktivists utilise a variety of technologies and online strategies to attain their goal which include:

1. **Anonymous Blogging:** Activists, whistleblowers, and journalists employ this tactic to voice opposition against regimes violating human rights or suppressing dissent. The platform's anonymity makes identifying the authors impossible.
2. **DoS and DDoS Attacks:** Hacktivists use these attacks to prevent access to targeted computer systems or networks by inundating them with traffic until they become inaccessible.
3. **Doxxing:** This involves gathering an individual's or organisation's information, often through hacking or social engineering, and making it public, typically involving highly sensitive data.
4. **Geobombing:** This technology allows internet users to add geotags to YouTube videos. Hacktivists employ geobombing to display the locations of videos posted by political prisoners and human rights activists on Google Earth and Google Maps.
5. **Leaking Information:** A common activist tactic where an individual within an organisation accesses and exposes highly sensitive or classified information about an individual, organisation, or government agency.
6. **RECAP:** The United States has a system called PACER (Public Access to Court Electronic Records) that provides fee-based access to federal court records. RECAP—which is PACER spelt backwards—

software enables users to search for free copies of these documents.

7. **Website Defacement:** Hacktivists alter a website's code or software to display messages conveying their viewpoint. These messages may be threatening or defamatory and can disable key functionality to deliver the hacktivist's message.
8. **Website Mirroring:** Hacktivists copy a legitimate website's content to another location with a slightly different URL, often used to circumvent censorship by blocking access to the original site by providing a mirrored copy.
9. **Website Redirects:** In this form of attack, hacktivists redirect users to another site promoting their cause.

Famous Hacktivist Groups

1. Hacktivismo

As mentioned earlier, the term 'hacktivism' was coined by the computer hacking group Cult of the Dead Cow. They are also the creators of the Back Orifice Remote Administration Tool (RAT), which gains remote access to machines running the Microsoft Windows operating system. Its parent organisation, CDC Communications, is affiliated with two other hacking groups known as Ninja Strike Force and Hacktivismo. Hacktivismo focuses on creating anti-censorship technology and contributed to giving the term 'hacker' a positive connotation.

2. Anonymous Group

Anonymous is a decentralised international hacktivist group known for cyberattacks against governments, government institutions, agencies, corporations, and the Church of Scientology. Their often-used motto is: 'We are unknown. We are legion. We forget nothing. We forgive no one—except ourselves.' After George Floyd's murder, Anonymous released videos, pictures, and other confidential documents exposing the brutality of American police.

3. Legion Hacktivist Group

Legion is a hacktivist group that attacked some of India's wealthiest and most powerful individuals by hacking their Twitter accounts. The group claims access to several email servers in India and encryption keys used by Indian banks. Legion made headlines in 2019 with a series of attacks targeting Rahul Gandhi, hacking not only his Twitter handle but also his email server. The next day, the Indian National Congress's Twitter was hacked, with irrelevant content tweeted. The gang later hacked Vijay Mallya, Barkha Dutt, and Raveesh Kumar's Twitter accounts as well. Between 2018 and 2020, Legion hacked a server of Russia's Federal Antimonopoly Service as the government attempted to censor the Telegram messaging app. While not causing significant harm, they posted a warning message to the Russian government.

4. WikiLeaks

Julian Assange launched the WikiLeaks website in 2006, through which many highly confidential documents of the American as well as other governments have been made public. A notable first step was the 2010 release of nearly 80,000 documents about the US war in Afghanistan, followed by the release of 400,000 more documents about the US war in Iraq. WikiLeaks later published 28,000 classified emails during the 2016 US presidential election.

5. Syrian Electronic Army

This group of Syrian hacktivists emerged in 2011, claiming to support Syrian President Bashar al-Assad. It was formed with the aim of protecting the Syrian government, computer networks, and defence systems and disrupting perceived threats to Syria. In 2013, they attacked several US government websites, unleashing the hoax that there had been an explosion at the White House and that the President had been injured.

6. LulzSec

In June 2011, members of the LulzSec group claimed responsibility for an attack on Sony Pictures, leaking data including names, passwords, email addresses, home addresses, and dates of birth of thousands of people. They were angered by Sony's legal action against George Hotz for hacking the PlayStation 3's software. The group threatened that this was the 'beginning of the end' for Sony and claimed to have hacked 10 million accounts, although Sony stated the real number was around 37,500.

Cyber Frauds That Shook the World

1. **The $100 Million Google and Facebook Spear Phishing Scandal**

   As far as we know, this fraud against two of the world's biggest companies, Google and Facebook, by a Lithuanian citizen named Ivaldas Rimasauskas is the biggest social engineering attack ever. The fraudsters tricked officials into believing they were computer manufacturers working for Google and Facebook. Both these companies had bought several products from the Taiwan-based company Quanta. Rimasauskas took advantage of this and sent a series of fake invoices to employees. He also created bank accounts in the name of this fake company. These scammers then sent phishing emails to specific Google and Facebook employees, invoicing them for services provided by Google and Facebook. Employees were instructed to deposit money into their fraudulent accounts as a result of the service. Between 2013 and 2015, Rimasauskas and his accomplices defrauded two tech giants out of $100 million.

Eventually, the fraud was discovered, and Facebook and Google took action through the US legal system. The attacker was arrested in Lithuania and extradited to the US, and as a result of legal proceedings, Facebook and Google were able to recover $49.7 million of the $100 million stolen from them.

2. **Targeting the US Department of Labour**

In this incident, the hackers created an email template that mimicked the look and feel of the US Department of Labour. These emails asked for the submission of bids for an ongoing project in this government department. These emails looked very professional and authentic due to which no one suspected that they were fake. This made unwary officials susceptible to being easily duped. The scam was intended to steal people's Microsoft Office login information. Additionally, the site would ask victims to reconfirm their login credentials once officials had recorded them. The scammers did this to reduce the risk of obtaining false credentials from careless input. This tactic proved to be highly effective.

3. **Russian Hacking Group Targets Ukraine with Spear Phishing**

   In February 2022, Microsoft issued a warning about a new spear phishing campaign by a Russian hacking group targeting Ukrainian government agencies and non-governmental organisations amidst rising tensions between Russia and Ukraine. The group, identified as Gameredon, has also been targeting organisations such as the police, ambulance, and fire force in Ukrainian territory since 2021.

   The attack involved sending spear phishing emails containing malware to trap the victim, with the emails also containing a tracking pixel to notify senders when emails are opened. This serves as a reminder of the important role that cybersecurity plays in international conflicts and the need for all organisations to improve their cybersecurity posture and protect against social engineering attacks.

4. **Sony Pictures Cyberattack**

   In 2014, Sony Pictures produced a Hollywood film called *The Interview,* which satirised the North Korean dictator. Following the release of the film, there was a cyberattack on Sony Pictures, which is believed to have been the work of the North Korean government. On November 24, an unknown group called Guardians of Peace hacked into the computer networks of Sony Pictures Entertainment, the parent company of Columbia Pictures. The hackers leaked several unreleased Sony Pictures movies, including *Annie, Mr Turner, Still Alice,* and *To Write Love on Her Arms.* The cyberattack also resulted in the theft of thousands of company files, including business contracts, financial records, and employee information. Moreover, hackers posted the movie *The Interview* online, in the public domain, before its release in theatres.

The attack was triggered by phishing emails that Sony employees received, which appeared to be emails from the Apple company. Interestingly, the North Korean government denied its involvement in the attack.

5. **Deepfake Attack on UK Energy Company**

In March 2019, the CEO of a UK energy provider received a phone call from someone who sounded like his boss. The voice was familiar, so he did not think there was any problem with the call. During the call, the CEO was asked to transfer $243,000 to a Hungarian supplier, which turned out to be a fraudster's bank account. This type of attack is known as a deepfake attack, where a fraudster uses artificial intelligence to create a fake picture, video, and audio media that convincingly mimic real people, often with the intent to deceive or manipulate viewers for malicious purposes.

In another instance, a Chinese aircraft parts maker called FACC lost nearly $60 million due to a CEO fraud attack. Criminals impersonated high-level executives and tricked employees into transferring funds. After the incident, FACC spent more money than it had lost by suing the CEO and CFO for allegedly failing to implement adequate internal security controls.

We will explore the phenomenon of Deepfake in more detail in the following section.

Deepfake: Don't Believe Your Eyes

Deepfake, a name which originates from the combination of deep learning and fake, is a technology that enables anyone with a computer and an internet connection to create realistic-looking photos and videos of any person Russia recently released a video in which Ukrainian President Zelensky appeared to be in favour of Russia and ready to surrender. However, this tactic failed miserably, as experts pinpointed its technical flaws, and the world realised that the video was fake. Some other examples of deepfake videos include one depicting President Obama using a specific term to describe former President Trump, another showing Mark Zuckerberg admitting that Facebook's real purpose is to exploit its users, and so forth. Deepfake videos are on the rise online and in the future, these videos will be absolutely flawless.

The most effective area where deepfake technology has been widely applied is, as with any technology, in pornography. As of September 2019, 96 per cent of deepfake videos online were pornographic. Websites using deepfake technology for pornography have been viewed by millions of people in the past two years alone.

Moreover, the artificial synthesis of videos involving famous celebrities or people you know directly can be dangerous. The use of deepfakes has begun to spread into the political realm, and the repercussions of this can be massive. Governments will now be able to disseminate fake videos that the entire nation may believe. It doesn't take much imagination to understand the severity of this issue. Imagine footage surfacing of a certain presidential candidate accepting bribes, engaging in sexual misconduct, or announcing a nuclear war. Additionally, due to the wide accessibility of the technology, such footage can be created by anyone—state-sponsored political groups, ordinary tech enthusiasts, or even children—against anyone.

What we need to do now is increase public awareness of the potential dangers of deepfakes. It is up to informed citizens to mount a critical defence against rampant fake news by verifying sources and promoting digital literacy. Only through collective vigilance can we mitigate the impact of this sophisticated form of deception.

Chapter 6

Sabotaging Selfies

Susanna Halleck, a teacher at Coral Springs Charter High School in Florida, went into labour unexpectedly. And while Susanna was writhing in pain, one of her students, Malik Waiter, thought it was a good idea to click a selfie. He asked his teacher to smile, but she refused. He still took a photo of her troubled face and posted it on social media, where it went viral.

In the past, character development took place through positive and negative feedback from friends, family, authorities, and locals in the real world. Would a teenager have thought to take a photo of their teacher in labour and publish it twenty or thirty years ago? The same year as the labour selfie incident, another controversial selfie went viral. A young woman with blonde hair, aviator sunglasses, and a white knit scarf and hat was out for a morning walk when she saw a man trying to hang himself from the Brooklyn Bridge. Instead of helping, she took a selfie in front of the tragic scene. Similar incidents have taken place worldwide, with many videos available on YouTube and other popular platforms.

The rapid rise of selfie culture, often without considering the context or the impact on others, highlights an issue that requires closer examination. In the following sections, we will delve into this phenomenon, exploring its underlying causes and the effects it has on society. We will also discuss potential solutions and strategies to address the negative aspects of selfie culture. Through this analysis, we aim to better understand how to balance self-expression with social awareness and empathy.

Kerala's Day of Shame

In 2010, on March 22, a bus overturned into the river at around 4 o'clock in Kottayam's Puthanangadi in Kerala. There was heavy rain and a strong flow in the river. Many passengers, including school children, were injured. Mothers wept bitterly as they waited for their children to return from school. A number of good locals, the police, and firefighters risked their lives and started the rescue operation. They worked together, praying that everyone could be saved before breathing their last.

The rescue operation was hampered more by the adverse conditions presented by the strong current in the river and the pouring rain. There was also a crowd that created a stampede and clamoured to capture the scene of the children fighting for their lives in the river on mobile phone cameras. The photo enthusiasts shouted at the police who obstructed the police and fire forces. Did these supposed intellectuals think that taking photos was more important than saving lives?

In the end, a request was made by the district collector through TV channels: 'If you have relatives watching these scenes, please call them back home. Don't obstruct the rescue operation.' While a group of men risked their lives to save the trapped children in the river, some people were blocking them and taking photos instead.

The negative effects of making videos and taking pictures in dire situations, as illustrated by the tragic bus accident in Kottayam, are profound. The actions of those who prioritised capturing the scene over aiding the rescue efforts not only hindered the lifesaving operations but also demonstrated a disturbing lack of empathy. This behaviour can delay critical assistance, increase the risk to victims and rescuers, and perpetuate a culture of insensitivity. Instead of helping, these individuals obstructed the police and firefighters, showing that the obsession with documenting events can overshadow the urgency of human compassion and action. It is crucial to recognise and address this issue, promoting a culture where aiding those in need takes precedence over the impulse to record and share traumatic events.

The Psychology Behind Selfies

Selfies allow individuals to express their identity, style, and personality, serving as a form of artistic expression or a way to showcase one's mood or emotions. They foster a sense of connection with friends, family, and followers, maintaining relationships and engagement. Receiving likes and positive comments on selfies can boost self-esteem and provide validation.

For some, selfies capture moments and experiences, creating visual memories of significant events or everyday life—simply documenting memories. Others do it to follow trends and feel part of the in-crowd.

Psychologically, taking selfies can activate the brain's reward system, releasing dopamine—a neurotransmitter associated with pleasure and satisfaction. This can lead to addiction as people seek that feeling of pleasure and validation. Social media platforms foster social comparison, where people evaluate their appearance, accomplishments, and lives against others, potentially causing feelings of inadequacy and low self-esteem, driving them to take more selfies for validation.

The real problem arises when people use selfies as a mode for gaining attention and admiration. They crave cyber attention, showcasing materialistic possessions like high-end cars. They believe their every move—what they eat, their education, celebrations, drinking habits, property, partner, children, and achievements—needs to be posted in real-time, fearing they will be forgotten otherwise. Some even develop a delusional belief that cyberspace exists solely for them and that all attention is focused on them.

Self-objectification occurs when people view themselves as objects to be looked at and evaluated rather than individuals with thoughts and experiences. The fear of missing out (FOMO) prompts individuals to take and share selfies to stay relevant and connected, as they consider social media a life-saving drug.

Narcissism, named after the Greek character Narcissus who fell in love with his reflection, is characterised by extreme selfishness, excessive self-confidence in appearance and abilities, and an indomitable desire for acceptance and love.

Evolutionary psychology suggests narcissism may have roots in self-awareness. In a famous study, great apes like chimpanzees, orangutans, and gorillas were placed in front of a mirror. Initially, they reacted as if another ape appeared, but after a few days, they realised the reflection was their own. They began exploring their bodies in the mirror, learning about parts they couldn't see without it. This 'passing the mirror test' suggests they have a self-concept—evidence of how they think, evaluate, and perceive themselves, exhibiting a distinct but consistent form of self-awareness.

The Perils of Selfie Culture

The widespread obsession with selfies has introduced various risks, both physical and mental. Let's explore some of the ways selfies can be harmful to us.

1. **Physical Danger**

   Seeking the perfect selfie can lead to accidents and injuries in dangerous locations. There have been numerous reports of people getting hurt or even dying while trying to capture selfies.

2. **Mental Health Issues**

   Constantly seeking validation through selfies can contribute to anxiety, depression, and low self-esteem, especially if expected social feedback is not received. Some individuals may develop an addiction to taking and posting selfies, which can interfere with daily life and relationships.

3. **Hiring Practices**

   Nowadays, companies often assess a candidate's online behaviour before making hiring decisions. Hiring managers may look for signs of narcissism in a candidate's social media presence, such as:

- Do they consistently stand out in their photos?
- Are they prominently featured in almost every photo?
- Do they frequently change their profile picture?
- When they post updates, do they primarily focus on themselves?

These considerations help hiring managers gauge a candidate's online persona and potential cultural fit within the organisation.

Promoting Healthy Selfie Habits

The first step is to set boundaries for your selfie behaviour. That includes limiting the time you spend on social media platforms. In that gained time, engage in activities that promote self-care, such as exercise, meditation, and spending time with people in the physical world.

Social media platforms can implement several features to discourage unhealthy selfie-taking behaviours and promote healthier online interactions:

1. Set a daily limit on the number of selfies a user can post. This can help prevent the pressure to constantly post new selfies and reduce the likelihood of unhealthy behaviours.
2. Implement a selfie-free mode that encourages users to take a break from selfie-taking and engage in other activities. This mode can be opt-in or set as a default for certain periods.

3. Use AI algorithms to detect patterns of unhealthy selfie-taking behaviours, such as excessive posting, using unrealistic filters, or extreme image editing. The platform can then warn users and provide resources for healthier interactions.
4. Designate certain areas or times as selfie-free zones, where users are discouraged from posting selfies. This can help create a culture where selfie-taking is not the primary focus of online interaction.
5. Encourage users to take breaks from the platform and engage in offline activities. This can promote a healthier balance between online and offline interactions.
6. Include a feature that allows users to shame or report others for posting excessive or inappropriate selfies but with utmost care. This can help create a culture where selfie-taking is discouraged and promote a healthier online environment.

Finally, there are apps available that track and limit social media usage, such as Freedom, SelfControl, and Moment. Additionally, built-in screen usage and app monitoring tools on Mac and Android platforms can help monitor your screen and app usage.

By following these steps, we can effectively balance our offline and online lives, ensuring that we maintain a healthy relationship with both digital and real-world environments. This approach allows us to prioritise meaningful interactions, manage screen time responsibly, and cultivate habits that promote overall well-being.

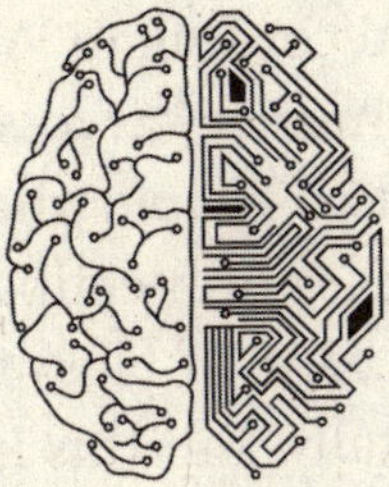

Chapter 7

Cyber Romance

The timeless principles of great love stories hinge on intimacy as the initial spark and separation as the fuel that keeps the fire burning. This is evident in classic tales like Tristan and Isolde, Romeo and Juliet, Scarlett and Rhett, and Nalan and Damayanti. However, in our modern era, technology plays an ever-growing role in mediating human contact and romance. Intimacy and sex between lovers have been revolutionised, with people easily finding and maintaining relationships online through social media, webcams, proximity apps, texting, sexting, and other innovative tools. These advancements offer endless possibilities for today's generation to connect and sustain their relationships.

The Illusion of Connection: How Online Interactions Blur Reality

There is a term called 'hyper personal interaction'. It is a term coined by communication expert Joseph Walther in 1996, at the dawn of the internet era, to describe the way individuals communicate online. According to Walther, connecting with people online has become very accessible and convenient.

Let's take the case of two people who meet online to explain this further. In most cases of meeting someone online, they do not see each other face-to-face in the beginning. Their relationship starts digitally. But this invisibility has no small effect on their relationship. Not seeing each other is not a disadvantage here, but rather an advantage. Mutual trust is essential for developing relationships. When communicating in cyberspace, this mutual trust is created only on the basis of the information that each person discloses. However, in the real world, we know how to judge the credibility of others. Handshakes, facial expressions, eye contact, differences in voice, posture, language, appearance, and smell are all taken into account by our brains knowingly or unknowingly. And so, we form an overall opinion about that person.

On traditional dating sites like Match.com and eHarmony, this meet-and-greet process is initially more arduous. You have to fill out a form and enter details such as personal information, job, age, place of birth, education level, income range, and your favourite books and movies. On these sites, artificial intelligence algorithms introduce two people to each other. People then decide whether profile photographs are attractive. If two people show that there is a spark between them, things will start to move forward.

In online dating, relationships progress very quickly through text messages, emails, chats, posts, etc. Even the emotional connection builds faster compared to relationships that start out in person. It can take months to develop that level of intimacy and feelings in a direct relationship. Psychologists call this paradox the 'stranger on the train syndrome'. You meet someone on a train journey and find yourself suddenly revealing your most personal information to this person you may never meet again.

There are two cyberpsychological phenomena at work here. One: the online disinhibition effect, i.e., the shedding of laziness, withdrawal, and social anxiety when entering the digital world. Two: Perceived anonymity, i.e., the feeling that they will never be seen or harmed. Due to these cyber effects, we expose a lot online. We never think that this partner who has never met us in real life will hurt us in any way. In our urgency to make a connection, we reveal the details of our lives to this stranger without hesitation. If our initial impression of someone is positive, things will then move quickly. In the cyber world, any void, gap, lack of complete information, ambiguity, etc., in communication is not a problem. Why? Here, our own brain fills the gap without us even knowing it in a way that suits us. If you get an impression of someone online, remember that it is not complete and realistic. Because you have filled in details about their personality, appearance, and character yourself and you are projecting a person you want in your mind onto the screen of your mind.

Modern psychology has theories which are relevant in explaining this phenomenon. A person often redirects some of their feelings or desires for another person to someone completely different. Freud called it 'transference'. You observe many characteristics of your father in the new boss of your organisation, and you attribute fatherly feelings to this new boss. We use these same psychological techniques to fill in gaps in the people we meet online.

Does this mean that the person you meet online is basically a fictional character? Are they just a figment of your own fantasy? Unfortunately, there is no way to say for sure. On a dating site, it is not two 'real' people trying to meet and mate, but two 'virtual' people. Yes, two cyber figures are interacting here. These are profiles that are deliberately made and moulded for a specific purpose. This is very far from reality. Princess Diana once said of her marriage that there were three of them. Online dating, on the other hand, involves four individuals: two real-world personalities and two cyber personalities.

But is it wise to reveal so much to someone else? The truth is that revealing your private details to complete strangers is sure to make you more vulnerable. Unnecessary and cruel criticism, accusations, teasing, bargaining, threats, and many other things may follow. The most problematic is when it crosses over into economic and sexual exploitation. Check out what Kaspersky, one of the most researched companies on cybersecurity, has to say in their report. 55 per cent of people who date online have experienced some form of bullying or harassment. This ranges from IT security breaches to meeting people in person who are completely different from their online profile. Statistics show that men make more mistakes than women. Twice as many male online daters said their laptop had been infected with malicious software, spyware, or ransomware after dating. And 13 per cent of men have received phishing emails trying to extort information from online dating sites, compared to just 7 per cent of women. Apart from this, men are also more likely to fall into the deliberate trap called honeypotting or honeytrapping.

Let's look at a recent report by the UK National Crime Agency (NCA). They say there has been a six-fold increase in rape crimes related to online dating in the past five years. Very quickly, people engage in sexist talk on dating sites, which can lead to false expectations. 71 per cent of these rapes took place on the first day of dating at either the victim's or the perpetrator's home. Furthermore, none of the perpetrators of this online dating harassment had a criminal history.

There is one thing widely accepted in military psychology: it is much easier to kill someone from a distance than up close. Confronting another person, attacking them directly, and witnessing their difficulties can cause a good deal of distress in humans. But telling people to push a button to harm people far away won't seem like a problem to most. The more you distance yourself from the people you hurt, the easier it is on your conscience. A survey showed that if you call a thousand people who eat chicken every day and ask if they can kill a chicken, not even three people would be willing. That's why in cyber dating, the distance between the suitors makes them more selfish, hurting their partner and not considering them human.

In conclusion, revealing personal details to someone met online can be perilous, exposing you to risks like identity theft, scams, and cyberstalking. Fraudsters often exploit personal information to gain access to financial accounts, create false identities, or manipulate victims into divulging even more sensitive data. Sharing intimate details with a stranger can also lead to emotional and psychological harm if that person uses the information for harassment or blackmail. The relative anonymity of the internet makes it easier for malicious individuals to present themselves as trustworthy, underscoring the crucial need to exercise caution and protect your personal information in online interactions.

Cyber-illicit Relationships

A young woman received a missed call one morning after she dropped her children off at school and finished other work. Curious about the unknown number, she called it back. It was a taxi driver, who was off duty and trying a number given by his friend at a recharge shop. With time, both persons connected with each other, and the relationship grew to the point where the woman was ready to leave her own children and husband to pursue this person from the missed call.

Let's take a look at another example. Anita, a software employee, was checking her Facebook at night when she saw a message from Jishnu, who had confessed his love for her during her undergraduate days. A one-line message 'Remember me?' took them back to their memories. Years later, the man who had proposed to Anita in her teenage years sought her out again. Jishnu was now in America, but the relationship grew from chats to phone calls. Later, when it progressed into direct encounters and sexual relations, the balance of the two families broke down. The case was settled before reaching the court.

Getting involved in an affair used to be very difficult. It took effort to find the right person, time, and occasion. In rural areas, this often meant sneaking around and hiding to advance love affairs. Overcoming the fear of maintaining illicit relationships involved dealing with moral and family policing, as well as police raids when sneaking into hotels and needing to return home before sunrise. Technology has made it easier to manage such relationships, allowing people to flirt from the comfort of their homes. With caution, these interactions can remain discreet, known only to the cyber-partners involved.

Society's mindset towards cyber-dating has also changed greatly. A growing number of sites and apps promote this, with homepages providing enticing reasons for why extra-marital relationships exist. There is now an attempt to justify and normalise adultery even in movies and other media forms. Apps like Hinge, Lavalife, Grindr, meet2cheat, Affairs Club, and Ashley Madison are designed specifically for short-term affairs and facilitating marital infidelity. However, these platforms harbour significant dangers. Many of them are involved in money laundering schemes that trap unsuspecting victims. In 2015, Ashley Madison's server was hacked, exposing the personal information of its 30 million users. This breach not only revealed private data and secrets but also provided a valuable resource for researchers in various fields, including psychology.

The hack exposed the most intimate details and images of hundreds of thousands of people. Analysts discovered that while 20 million men sent messages on the site, only 1,492 women did, indicating the widespread use of female chatbots. The exposure of this highly private information led to numerous divorces and separations. The repercussions didn't stop there—thousands of people were blackmailed, and many even committed suicide. In countries like Pakistan, where adultery is illegal, eight thousand Ashley Madison users faced severe consequences, including imprisonment. The false sense of anonymity provided by the cyber world led many to take risks they otherwise wouldn't have.

Another important point to note is that cybercrime ethics is a rapidly evolving field, and its interpretation varies significantly across different countries. Sexting, lewd Facebook posts, and other displays of infidelity are not considered adultery in the UK and Canada, whereas, in the United States, excessive time spent online for cyber dating or gaming can be used in court to show a history of poor parenting and affect custody decisions.

So, we can see that one may not be able to call cyber infidelity adultery in the broadest sense but that doesn't mean cyberbullying isn't a serious breach of trust. This small pleasure has far-reaching consequences. Searching for love online in order to save time, money, and energy can seriously affect the bond of family life. Multiple studies show excessive social network use by a partner creates jealousy and increases alienation. Giuseppe Castro of Italy beheaded his wife after suspecting her of an online affair, telling police, 'She was always chatting with other men. I couldn't bear it.'

To summarise, the evolution of cyber-dating has brought about significant shifts in societal attitudes, normalising behaviours once considered taboo. Platforms catering to extramarital relationships highlight the complexities and dangers inherent in online interactions, from privacy breaches to legal implications across different jurisdictions. As cyber-dating continues to reshape relationship dynamics, it underscores the critical need for individuals to navigate these digital spaces cautiously, mindful of the profound impacts on personal lives and societal norms alike.

The Comfort of Virtual Love

The emergence of virtual girlfriends has sparked widespread fascination and debate. These digital companions offer a unique form of emotional support and companionship, challenging traditional notions of intimacy and relationships. These virtual girlfriends are programmed to never leave you, and they don't require much attention. To the shock of social psychologists, many people have declared their love for these virtual girlfriends to be real because of the comfort and support these digital girlfriends provide. Even an anthropologist who specialises in Japanese popular culture, Patrick Galbraith, has said that 'one's relationship with a Love Plus character is a real relationship.' Love Plus is a Japanese video game series marketed as a dating simulator that helps individuals learn how to be in a relationship. Since its launch in 2010, Love Plus has attracted hundreds of thousands of players worldwide, from boys and girls of middle-school age to adults, who have become die-hard fans of this game. One major attraction of the game is that it doesn't come with the headaches that come with a real-life relationship.

While Love Plus and similar virtual girlfriend simulations offer a novel escape from the complexities of real-life relationships, they also raise profound questions about the nature of human connection and emotional fulfilment. As technology continues to blur the lines between the virtual and the real, it is essential to critically examine the impact of these digital relationships on individuals and society as a whole.

Cyber-celibacy: A Growing Threat to the World

A survey released by the Japanese government has revealed some alarming findings for Japan. As we know, reproduction is a fundamental factor in the survival process of any species, and its driving force is passion and sex. However, the availability of digital girlfriends like Rinko, Manaka, and Nene threatens this survival process. In Japan, there is a growing concern about the high number of single Japanese men and women of marriageable age who have no interest in finding a love partner. They often describe real relationships as 'annoying'. This concern is particularly present in Japan, where about 40 per cent of men and women of marriageable age are single.

Another survey found that one in four unmarried J apanese men in their thirties have never had sex. A social psychology researcher has noted that: 'In Japanese society, they have a lot of entertainment beyond love and sex, such as anime, celebrities, comics, games, and sports. Why should they choose love or sex when there are other fun things that don't involve pain and suffering?' This combination of the illusion of real-world relationships and the Japanese people's general fear of failure has created a serious social problem. If current trends continue, the government fears that by 2060, Japan's population will shrink by more than 30 per cent.

This threat of cyber-celibacy is not limited to Japan. Surveys conducted in India indicate that face-to-face interactions and true love between individuals are steadily declining. The fact is that more and more people are forgetting how to interact with others and losing the ability to do so. Furthermore, a heightened fear of failure in real-world relationships, a desire to avoid the pain of real relationships, troubled marriages that bounce from relationship to relationship, infidelity, and subsequent problems or legal entanglements drive people to pursue virtual relationships.

There is also evidence showcasing that dating apps, sexting, and other virtual encounters may actually have a negative impact on people's sex lives. Dr Craig Malkin, a clinical psychologist at Harvard Medical School, says that this technology itself makes us reluctant to connect with each other in the real world.

The science behind this is that our brains don't differentiate between joy, comfort, or stimulation derived from real-life experiences and those from virtual sources. The brain just seeks pleasure, regardless of its origin. And though gaming and pornography cannot cure loneliness, they can fulfil our need for dopamine—the happiness hormone—which can become highly addictive over time. As a result, humans move away from their fellow creatures and take refuge in cyberspace.

Online dating offers convenience and efficiency in connecting with potential partners, but it is essential to understand the risks, especially regarding sharing personal information with strangers. Revealing private details to unfamiliar individuals can leave you susceptible to exploitation, such as economic or sexual exploitation. Thus, in order to safeguard yourself, exercise caution when using online dating platforms. Protect your personal information, approach online interactions with vigilance, and familiarise yourself with signs of potential exploitation. These precautions are crucial for ensuring a safe and successful online dating experience.

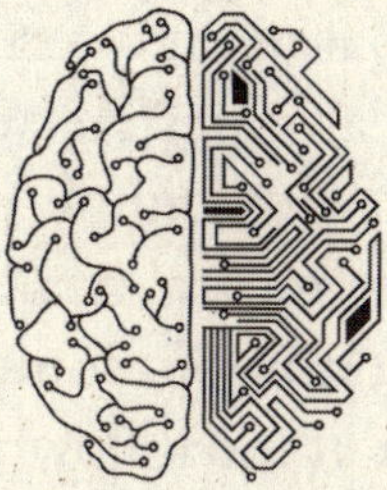

Chapter 8

The Rise of Cyberchondria

Imagination is a powerful tool that has played a crucial role in human evolution. Evolutionary scientists believe it served a vital purpose for our ancestors by allowing them to foresee potential dangers, such as imagining a tiger lurking in the bushes. This ability to anticipate threats helped ensure their survival in the wild, where danger was a constant presence. As a result, those who used their imagination to predict and avoid threats were more likely to survive and pass on their genes.

However, the misuse of imagination can lead to the fabrication of unfounded fears, which in turn can heighten our anxiety and fear. For instance, in the past, we only visited a doctor when symptoms were severe enough to warrant the effort and cost. But nowadays, at the first sign of a symptom, people turn to Google, which introduces a different set of problems. Many people arrive at hospitals overwhelmed by fear from what they have read online about their symptoms. Doctors frequently encounter patients armed with self-diagnosed conditions based on internet searches. These self-diagnosed symptoms can interfere with accurate diagnosis. The same issue arises with online psychometric tests and self-diagnosis of serious mental health issues. Patients come in convinced of their condition, sometimes claiming to have rare diseases. Let's look at the following example:

A doctor friend of mine recently had a patient insisting he had infectious river blindness, a disease only found among Amazonian tribes. The doctor had a hard time convincing the patient that he could not possibly have this disease. Instead of being relieved, the patient was disappointed that his grandiose diagnosis was incorrect. This example highlights the negative effects of self-diagnosis and the importance of professional medical evaluation.

Let's look at another example. Imagine your nose is bleeding. You search on Google and find many possible reasons for the situation, such as dry air, a stuffy nose, acute sinusitis, allergies, aspirin use, bleeding disorders like haemophilia, blood thinners (anticoagulants) such as warfarin and heparin, use of chemicals like ammonia, cocaine use, leukaemia, and so on. If a patient with these symptoms rules out all other possibilities and decides they have leukaemia, it can be a cause for concern.

Self-diagnosis and treatment have become a global issue. An international survey was conducted to understand the percentage of people who search for their symptoms on the internet. The results revealed that in China, 94 per cent of people searched for their symptoms online, while in Thailand, it was 93 per cent, in Saudi Arabia, it was 91 per cent, and in India, it was 90 per cent.

The inclination to self-diagnose using online information often results in unnecessary anxiety and misdiagnosis. For instance, interpreting a common symptom like a nosebleed as a sign of a severe illness like leukaemia underscores the importance of seeking professional medical advice rather than relying solely on internet resources. In the next section, we will explore hypochondriasis, a condition characterised by excessive concern about having a serious illness, even in the absence of medical evidence and significant symptoms.

Hypochondriasis

Until recently, hypochondriasis, marked by excessive health concerns, garnered significant attention. However, in the Diagnostic and Statistical Manual of Mental Disorders, Fifth Edition (DSM-5), approximately 75 per cent of what was previously labelled hypochondria has been reclassified under the new diagnostic category of somatic symptom disorder. The remaining 25 per cent now falls under illness anxiety disorder.

People with hypochondria often think there is something seriously wrong with them and may even believe they have undiagnosed diseases. They perceive their symptoms and physical disorders as indications of a serious illness, and they may consider themselves as medical experts. They search and read articles related to medical subjects and health magazines and books as well as repeatedly watch medical programs like *Ask the Doctor* and scientific and non-scientific YouTube videos. They constantly seek medical advice and make frequent hospital visits, where the staff conducts all necessary tests. However, their anxiety and worry persist even after a doctor's assurance that there are no real physical problems. They may feel frustrated that no one has yet discovered the disease they believe they have.

Another characteristic of the hypochondriac is distrust of the medical profession and an urge to question the doctor's authority and knowledge. They think they know better than the doctor and may consult many doctors within a short period. Most doctors consider such people to be nuisances and a waste of time for other patients. When a doctor finally tells a patient they have hypochondriasis, it can lead to further frustration and distress. Estimates suggest that 4 to 9 per cent of people have hypochondria, and it is equal in men and women. Such people often suffer from various emotional difficulties, such as anxiety or depression.

Munchausen Syndrome

Munchausen syndrome is a condition in which a person deliberately presents themselves with illnesses or symptoms and pretends to be sick when visiting a doctor. The background of this condition is interesting. During the 18th century, Emperor Peter I of Russia was engaged in a war against the Ottoman Turks. Baron Karl Friedrich Hieronymus Freiherr von Munchausen was a mercenary in the Russian army. After the war ended and he was out of work, he called his friends for a drinking party. Along with liquor, he also indulged in tales of his military adventures—super-adventure stories that had no connection to the truth. Rudolph Eric Raspe, a fraud scholar, saw this as an opportunity and self-published a book titled, *An Account of the Marvelous Voyages of Baron Munchausen*. Munchausen's stories were further spiced up by the writer who added his own touch.

This book was a huge success, and British doctor Richard Asher coined the name 'Munchausen syndrome' to refer to patients presenting with dramatically fabricated symptoms. In the UK, people with Munchausen-type syndrome are sometimes referred to as 'hospital addicts'. Such people are much rarer than hypochondriacs and are generally not on good terms with members of the medical profession. Some people develop this condition after being hospitalised for an underlying illness. They lie about a disease they don't have and get an emotional thrill out of fooling the doctors. They also thoroughly enjoy the thought of intellectually deceiving others.

Later, paediatrician Roy Meadow classified individuals who falsely claim their children have illnesses they do not actually have as suffering from 'Munchausen syndrome by proxy'. Individuals with this syndrome are a nuisance to medical professionals. Research indicates that in 93 per cent of cases, mothers have claimed their children had specific illnesses and sought hospitalisation. Dr Meadow coined this behaviour, recounting instances such as a woman mixing her own blood into her child's urine to feign illness, and another case where a mother overdosed her toddler with black pepper, causing sickness.

In one of the most severe cases of this syndrome, Kathy Bush, a woman from Florida suffering from Munchausen syndrome by proxy, inflicted serious harm on her 12-year-old daughter, Jennifer. Jennifer was admitted to the hospital two hundred times, undergoing forty surgeries. The child was poisoned multiple times. Kathy Bush was arrested in 1999, and her daughter was placed in foster care out of state, where she received the necessary medical attention and showed improvement in her health.

If we delve deeper into the underlying causes, we will find that individuals with Munchausen syndrome manipulate others to gain approval, attention, and sympathy. In countries like Canada, some exploit this syndrome to secure free accommodation, government benefits, medications, and financial aid. However, the primary motivation often lies deeper. Some seek to position themselves as heroes in the eyes of others, especially when caring for chronically ill children, which drives them to commit these heinous acts.

Internet Munchausen: From Deception to Digital Sympathy

The Munchausen syndrome of the internet is a natural evolution of this condition. It provides a more efficient and rewarding environment for such people's ploys. They can quickly get the sympathy of hundreds of people online, especially women. The sympathy people pour out online is twice as much as the momentary sympathy they might get from a doctor after waiting hours at the hospital. Instead of fooling a small circle of friends, neighbours, and medical professionals, they can fool thousands of people in a single day.

Let's look at a shocking example of Munchausen on the internet. This is the story of a blogger named David Rose, who was known as Dave on Wheels. The blogger revealed on Facebook that he lives in Los Angeles and is totally deaf, suffers from cerebral palsy, and has lost mobility from the neck down. Between 2008 and 2012, he garnered followers on Twitter and Facebook with his heart-wrenching stories. As he gained more and more attention, Kim Kardashian and other celebrities retweeted David's sad thoughts and described him as 'synonymous with survival'. He was getting tons of likes, comments, love, affection, and compassion.

Just then, news breaks that David has passed away from pneumonia. His sister, Nicole Rose, shared this heartbreaking update on her Facebook wall. The conclusion of the Dave on

Wheels saga devastated thousands of followers, flooding his page with condolences. The truth finally emerged when a dedicated fan arrived in Los Angeles for the funeral, only to discover that Dave was a fictional character created by Nicole Rose. Dave was a persona crafted to garner love and live a more fulfilling life in the eyes of others.

Furthermore, it is important to note that these issues are not confined to America alone. In Kerala, renowned writers have documented their struggles with delusional disorders. Similarly, across cyberspace, many individuals garner sympathy and followers by sharing fabricated experiences unrelated to reality. Today, some of these individuals have become influential social media figures with thousands of followers.

The main takeaway here is that imagination is a potent force, capable of crafting entire worlds and scenarios effortlessly. Yet, when the line between reality and fantasy blurs, the consequences can be profound. Clinical hallucination and delusional disorder illustrate this, where individuals' imaginations become so vivid and convincing that they start believing their own fabrications. Some may even share these tales on social media, garnering large followings and unwittingly spreading misinformation.

The crux of the issue lies in these narratives being detached from reality, yet their allure can sway many into believing their authenticity. This sets off a perilous cycle of deceit, trapping individuals in their own delusions while confusing and misinforming others. This phenomenon underscores the critical need for fact-checking and cultivating critical thinking in our digital era. It serves as a stark reminder that not everything encountered on social media is inherently true.

Chapter 9

The Digital Underworld

The Hidden Abyss: Unraveling the Secrets of the Deep Web

The deep web is a significant topic in law enforcement and cybersecurity, referring to an unindexed portion of the internet that far exceeds the size of the commonly accessed surface web. Specifically, it comprises 96 to 99 per cent of all online content, including data from US government databases, medical libraries, university records, classified cell phone data, and email histories. Similar to the surface web, content on the deep web can be shared with others, but it remains inaccessible via standard browsers and requires specialised tools for navigation.

One of the fundamental features of the deep web is its ability to facilitate anonymous content sharing, ensuring confidentiality by concealing your identity and location without leaving traceable evidence such as your computer's IP address. Unlike the surface web, which is accessible through mainstream browsers like Chrome or Safari, the deep web necessitates specialised tools like TOR (The Onion Router) for access, as its sites are not indexed.

The deep web was first used by the US government and the protocols for the TOR browser were initially developed using funds from the US federal government. It was originally designed for counterintelligence agents and political dissidents to communicate securely and anonymously and served as a crucial tool for protecting the identities of individuals who required anonymity. However, the anonymity provided by the deep web led to the creation of a digital black market which has been flourishing since 2002 when the TOR software was made available for free download.

Today, the deep web has transformed in form, appearance, and intent. It now mirrors the lawless pirate havens of the Caribbean during the 17th and 18th centuries—a vast and uncharted territory where cybercriminals operate with impunity, beyond the reach of conventional jurisdictional regulations. Limited legal frameworks pose minimal hindrances to their activities. Moreover, legitimate platforms like Amazon and Netflix are also accessible within this realm. But the primary draw lies in the fact that the deep web hosts a thriving online black market where illegal goods and services can be easily and efficiently traded. Here, one can procure a range of criminal services, from extortion and murder-for-hire to prostitution and various scams. This shadowy realm supports a robust criminal underworld teeming with terrorist networks, criminal syndicates, drug traffickers, contract killers, and purveyors of child pornography.

But how do such rampant illegal activities thrive on the deep web and is there no way to curb them? This dilemma poses a significant challenge for countries worldwide. The sheer scale and reach of this underground network present formidable obstacles. Within this uncharted realm, there are countless hiding spots and illicit sites frequently shift to new domains with transient addresses. These platforms also refrain from conventional payment methods like traceable credit cards or PayPal, opting instead for virtual currencies such as Bitcoin. This further complicates law enforcement efforts to monitor and regulate these activities effectively.

Dark Web Marketplaces: Crime in the Digital Shadows

The dark web's shadowy marketplaces operate beyond the reach of law enforcement and traditional monitoring, offering a vast array of illegal goods and services—from drugs and weapons to hired assassins. This article explores these sinister marketplaces and the various ways they facilitate real-world crime.

Among the most prominent are drug trading sites peddling everything from marijuana to heroin. These platforms employ tactics like discount sales, coupon codes, and buy-one-get-one-free offers to lure customers. Some even provide escrow services, holding payment until packages arrive safely, and offering after-sales support and service for technical issues. Europol categorises such sites as 'crime as a service' (CaaS) providers. Another hot commodity is stolen credit information or 'dumps'. These sites guarantee refunds for faulty data and provide fraud tutorials.

The incorporation of cryptocurrencies like Bitcoin and Monero enables these marketplaces' operations. Such untraceable digital currencies cloak criminals in anonymity, while encryption obstructs law enforcement monitoring of communications and site operator tracking.

The dark web's labyrinthine marketplaces represent a fascinating, disturbing rabbit hole—from the menagerie of illegal offerings to their marketing tactics. As we navigate the digital world's challenges, staying informed about these shadowy corners' potential dangers is critical. While authorities work to combat such activities, anonymity and encryption make it an immense undertaking, necessitating ongoing efforts to disrupt and dismantle these illegal enterprises.

Pirate Bay: A Controversial Legacy of Crime and Public Good

As discussed earlier, platforms like the deep web often appear to be solely associated with criminal activities. However, there are instances where actions considered criminal from one perspective can be viewed as beneficial to the public or the world at large from another angle. The story of Pirate Bay exemplifies this dichotomy.

Software piracy refers to the unauthorised copying, distribution, or use of software without proper licensing. Pirate Bay was notorious for facilitating free downloads of games, videos, movies, songs, books, and apps via torrent files. Founded in 2003 by Swedish activists, the site's creators claimed their aim wasn't content theft or criminality, but rather to challenge what they viewed as a corrupt capitalist market. One of its founders, Ross Ulbricht, emphasised their intent was to disrupt the established economic order.

After extensive efforts, the Swedish government successfully shut down Pirate Bay, the world's largest piracy site, on 10 December 2014. A surprise raid by the Swedish police in Stockholm led to the site's servers being seized, causing Pirate Bay to abruptly disappear from the internet.

Despite this shutdown, the site continues to resurface under various new names and domains.

Digital Piracy in India

The digital age has brought a tidal wave of piracy crashing upon creative industries worldwide. India, ranking third globally for visits to illegal video streaming sites, has felt this stark rise acutely. Piracy's impact ripples through multiple facets—disrupting original creations, impacting livelihoods, and causing devastating revenue losses.

Several factors fuel India's piracy surge. Access to cheap or free content entices many, while new technology proliferates pirated material to those previously geographically restricted. The Covid-19 pandemic amplified demand further, with film piracy skyrocketing 62 per cent amid lockdowns.

The allure of easily accessible pirated entertainment comes at a heavy cost. Beyond monetary losses, rampant piracy stifles creativity and innovation—the driving forces behind India's burgeoning arts and entertainment industries. Preserving these cultural cornerstones requires a multi-pronged approach targeting both supply and demand.

The Need for Stronger Intellectual Property Laws

Piracy takes a staggering toll on the creative industry. The television and film sectors alone support millions of jobs, making rampant counterfeiting a direct threat to revenues and employment. In India, awareness of piracy's illegalities remains dismal, and a lack of robust legal infrastructure hinders compliance checks. Existing laws like the Copyright Act, 1957 are riddled with loopholes, rendering enforcement an uphill battle.

Implementing stringent intellectual property (IP) and copyright laws to safeguard creators and their content has become an urgent imperative. IP laws are crucial not just for legal experts, but all stakeholders involved in content creation and facilitation. Formulating a comprehensive IPR framework is also necessary to bolster India's global IP ranking, currently a paltry 43 out of 55 countries. In the intensely competitive global market vying for investment in creativity, India's natural advantages position it to reap immense gains from a strengthened IP environment.

Adherence to newer laws like the National Intellectual Property Rights (IPR) Policy 2016 and the establishment of cyber digital crime units remain fledgling efforts. Lacking adequate legislation, courts have been limited to issuing John Doe orders and dynamic injunctions—mere stop-gaps. Robust enforcement of existing laws and regulations is imperative to combating the scourge of digital piracy.

The music and movie industries in India face an existential threat from digital piracy. A lack of awareness coupled with inadequate laws has allowed this menace to fester, inflicting revenue losses and reputational harm on creators. It is critical that the government and stakeholders join forces to implement stronger intellectual property protections and enhance enforcement measures, safeguarding the creative industry. By doing so, India can fortify its IP environment, stimulate investment in creativity, and propel the growth of its music and movie sectors.

Chapter 10

Phones and Relationships

Entertainment 24x7

Did you know that we touch our phones an average of 2,600 times a day? Since the Covid-19 pandemic, the average Indian spends around 7 hours daily staring at a screen. Endless scrolling through social media, watching YouTube videos, sifting through memes and shared content, and constantly checking WhatsApp statuses and Instagram stories have made it almost impossible to put down our phones. But have you ever thought about how smartphone addiction is affecting your life?

Several studies have shown that constant phone usage significantly impacts mental and psychological health and also disrupts studies, work, business, hobbies, and relationships. These effects are even more pronounced in children. For instance, separation anxiety disorder, primarily seen in children, involves an intense fear of being away from a loved one or cherished object, making it difficult for them to think about anything else. This anxiety now extends to their phones. When told to put their phones away, many children become irritable and upset, experiencing both mental and physical stress. Additionally, too much phone usage " diseases of the eyes, waist, neck, etc. On the other hand, mental disturbances, dizziness, and insomnia can also occur. Moreover, adults are not much better off, often experiencing similar separation anxiety from their phones.

The important point to note here is that the phone has undeniably become an addiction. This pervasive issue demands attention, as it impacts our well-being and daily lives more profoundly than we might realise. Addressing this addiction is crucial for improving mental health and fostering healthier habits in our increasingly digital world.

Phubbing: How Cell Phones Threaten Personal Relationships

A few years back, I presented a seminar on cyberpsychology at one of Kerala's most prestigious institutes of higher learning. Five minutes into the seminar, a teacher entered the hall, absorbed in his phone. He sat in the middle of the room among the students and didn't look up from his phone for the next hour. Ironically, as I discussed the psycho-social problems caused by phones, he exemplified the very issue. His behaviour, driven by cell phone and social media addiction, was rude and disrespectful, especially in front of the students.

Phubbing, a term recently added to the Oxford Dictionary, was coined by the Macquarie Dictionary of Australia in 2012. It describes the act of interacting with one's digital friends in cyberspace while ignoring those physically present. Similar to how alcohol and drugs can make people forget themselves and act inappropriately, cell phone addiction can lead to harmful behaviours. It is crucial for us to recognise that when technology interferes with human relationships, it creates wounds in both social connections and mental health.

This phenomenon is most evident within families, where the cell phone has become the main villain. Husbands and wives are more focused on social media interactions, seeking comments and likes on their pictures, rather than appreciating the small joys, harmonies, privations, and jokes in their relationships. Such intimate moments, playful conversations, and emotional connection between husband and wife are increasingly being disrupted by cell phones and social media. And by the time they realise that their attention to nurturing their digital identities is undermining their family security, it may be too late. Additionally, even children struggle to form strong connections with their parents, as everyone is constantly glued to their phones.

In conclusion, the pervasive use of cell phones and social media is eroding the fabric of our personal relationships and mental well-being. And though it might seem that our cell phones have drawn us in so deeply that it is impossible to break free. By recognising and addressing this addiction holistically, we can foster healthier, more meaningful interactions with those around us. So, the next time your friend is engrossed in their phone instead of talking to you, be bold and say, 'Will you please stop this phubbing?'

The Digital Divide in Modern Relationships

Are you in love with your smartphone? In a study conducted by two prestigious universities in the United States, 75 per cent of women rated cell phones as a major factor influencing their family life in the wrong direction. In another survey conducted in France, 27 per cent of young women said they are willing to give up sex to use cell phones and Facebook. Similarly, in India, a survey by Ipsos revealed that 31 per cent of respondents share this sentiment. But the more interesting, yet shocking, revelations were made by young women in Britain. 23 per cent of young women revealed that they browse Facebook even during intimate settings.

These statistics show that face-to-face interactions in the community are drastically reduced. Fumbling on the phone between conversations and serious discussions has also become a common occurrence. Moreover, the influence of smartphones and social media on intimate relationships is evident across various cultures, highlighting a concerning shift in priorities and interactions.

To summarise, as technology continues to shape our interactions, the challenge lies in balancing the benefits of connectivity with the preservation of meaningful face-to-face communication. Recognising these dynamics is crucial in navigating the complexities of modern relationships and fostering healthier digital habits for the future.

Mobile Phone Addiction: A Cross-Generational Challenge

One evening, a young man called me. He is a software engineer and started speaking anxiously, 'Sir, I am fed up with this mobile phone addiction. They are always on their phones, even while eating. Even when they meet and talk to us, they have mobile phones in their hands. You can see them searching for something or watching countless videos throughout the entire day. What should I do, sir?'

This question is all too familiar but there is a twist in this story. Usually, it is parents who worry about their children's mobile phone addiction but in this case, the young man was concerned about his parents' addiction to mobile phones. This is not an isolated incident. From toddlers to teenagers to adults, everyone is glued to their mobile phones. And like the younger generation likes photos on Instagram, chatting, and sharing memes, many elderly people spend their time forwarding messages, treating WhatsApp as an encyclopedia, and watching all kinds of online content.

In today's digital era, mobile phones exert an all-pervasive influence across generations, captivating both the young and old. The software engineer's concern over his parents' mobile addiction highlights a broader societal issue, underscoring how ubiquitous and ingrained this technology has become in our daily lives, shaping behaviours and interactions. Whether toddlers engrossed in educational apps, teenagers navigating social media's labyrinth, or adults consuming copious online content, the mobile's allure defies age barriers. This phenomenon necessitates a reflection on managing our digital habits while maintaining meaningful connections in an increasingly connected yet paradoxically isolating world. Striking a balance between leveraging technology's benefits and preserving genuine human interaction is essential for fostering healthier relationships and lifestyles amidst the digital transformation.

Guidelines for Healthy Phone Habits

As we have covered earlier, phone usage naturally increases if you use your smartphone for work as well as general purposes. Email, notepad, Uber, voice recorder, bank apps, etc. come within the natural range of use. However, we must remember that none of us are immortal and that our days are limited. Instead of wasting time scrolling through trivial information, following celebrities' private lives, or obsessing over the curated, photoshopped achievements people post on social media, we should focus on making the most of our time. Engaging in these distractions only destroys our peace and negatively impacts our work and relationships.

De-addiction expert and renowned psychologist, Dr Kimberly Yang, advises to take a 'digital detox' every weekend. That means plugging your phone into its charger and leaving it there on Saturday and Sunday. Stay away from digital devices for at least 48 hours. Even Pope Francis says that Christmas is a time for putting your phones away.

Danny Berry, one of the pioneers in the invention of computers and online gaming, commented, 'Honey, no one would say on their deathbed, "I wish I had spent more time alone at my computer."'

All in all, we need to be e clear about social media usage when reviewing app usage. Find out the usage of Facebook, WhatsApp, Snapchat, Instagram, Twitter, etc. There are many applications that can clearly monitor your phone usage and give you statistics so that you can better manage your phone usage. AppTym, Quality Time, App Usage and many other apps are examples of this.

Chapter 11

Social Manipulation

Frances Haugen, a former Facebook employee, revealed some shocking pieces of information to the world in 2021. Haugen is an American data engineer, scientist, and product manager who received her Master of Business Administration from Harvard Business School in 2011. She is also a whistleblower, meaning she disclosed private information that was considered illegal, unethical, affecting security, or fraudulent in the organisation she worked for.

In 2015, Haugen joined Yelp as a data product manager, focused on enhancing search through image recognition. After a year, she transitioned to Pinterest. Motivated by a close person's online radicalisation in 2019, Haugen joined Facebook with the aim of contributing to a better, less toxic platform. Seeing potential in Facebook to bring out the best in people, she expressed interest in a role related to misinformation, consequently becoming a product manager on the Facebook civic integrity team. However, following the 2020 US elections, Facebook dissolved its civic integrity team, sowing seeds of disillusionment in Haugen. Observing a recurring pattern of Facebook prioritising profit over public safety, she decided to become a whistleblower and departed in May 2021.

That spring, Haugen reached out to John Tye, founder of the pro bono law firm Whistleblower Aid, who agreed to represent her and protect her anonymity. By late summer 2021, she began meeting with US Congress members, including Senators Richard Blumenthal and Marsha Blackburn. In 2021, she disclosed tens of thousands of Facebook internal documents to the Securities and Exchange Commission and *The Wall Street Journal.* When Facebook recruited her from Google, she made it clear that she was only interested in working in a role that removed misinformation. In 2019, she was promoted to product manager on Facebook's civic integrity team. In the days that followed, she clearly understood the inaction of the Facebook company on the issue of countering misinformation and left the company in May 2021. But weeks before her resignation, she had downloaded thousands of internal documents from the company's computers. She left there determined to expose the company's immorality to the world.

This complex and weighty matter required collective effort, beyond the capability of any single individual to analyse alone. Hence, 17 other news organisations united to form a consortium for this initiative. American media giants such as the *Washington Post, New York Times, Associated Press, Atlantic, Reuters, The Wire,* and *CNN* were part of this consortium. Additionally, several European news agencies joined forces with them. Together, they meticulously analysed these documents and brought forth their revelations to the public, under the project name 'Facebook Papers'.

For more than a decade, Facebook has been the world's most dominant online platform. It currently has more than 2.8 billion monthly users, a presence in more than 190 countries, and the facility to post content in more than 160 languages. However, it has become a wholesale breeding ground for hate speech, inflammatory rhetoric, and misinformation, and their efforts to curb this trend have been ineffective. As a result, Facebook faced serious allegations, accused of promoting hate speech and violence. Moreover, there were claims that the platform indirectly supported terrorist groups in various countries globally. The algorithms used by Facebook have been implicated in sparking riots and violence in numerous locations worldwide.

The key takeaway is that a social media platform intended to unite people is, in reality, dividing them. The divisiveness and extremism evident today are only the beginning, and without swift action, the situation could escalate. Mark Zuckerberg's acknowledgement that Facebook contributes to misinformation and his steps to address it lends credence to these allegations.

Frances Haugen brought all these allegations to the world's attention by leaking thousands of Facebook internal documents. She filed eight complaints against Facebook with the US Securities Exchange Commission. She also said she did not intend to defame Facebook with this disclosure and urged Facebook to acknowledge these issues, take them seriously, and take immediate action.

I will conclude this section with the words of Frances Haugen: 'I have worked on four different types of social networks. I understand how complex and subtle the problems are. The way Facebook is doing it, in particular, is extremely destructive. We are asking for changes in

Facebook for the sake of our children, public safety, privacy, and the protection of democracy. Because of this unethical Facebook algorithm, democracy is literally at risk all over the world. Children are at risk, and violence is spreading globally.'

Facebook Papers

Let's look at some of the details revealed in the Facebook papers. In February 2019, researchers created a dummy account on social media to try to understand the experience of an average Indian user. Facebook algorithms recommend a number of things for users to watch. The recommendations these researchers saw were shocking. For three weeks, its news feed was filled with fake news and hate speech. Facebook's algorithm was recommending violence, beheading photos and dead bodies to the user.

Can you fathom why such hateful and violent content is so precisely chosen and fed into one's mind? In February 2019, during the Pulwama attack, it became evident that the spread of this hatred was intricately linked to the incident. Indians were bombarded with hateful and violent posts against Pakistan, with numerous fake news images circulating at that time. During those days, posts containing extremely abusive language against the people of Pakistan were being shared despite having no relation to the attack. The same thing was happening in Pakistan, where anti-Indian messages were being spread. However, if you intentionally avoid such content, leave it unliked, and ignore it, the next weapon in their arsenal will be deployed. Facebook's algorithm will begin suggesting pornographic content to you.

In response, a Facebook spokesperson stated, 'Facebook always strives to minimise hate messages on our platform.

Since this report came out, we have made changes to Facebook's algorithm to further improve these systems.'

It is important not to assume that their statements are entirely justified. While it is true that Facebook has taken some measures after recognising these issues, researchers have found that the changes made have had little impact on the improvements Facebook claims to have implemented. While they have set aside a significant amount of money to combat misinformation, fake news, and hate speech, 87 per cent of this budget is allocated to a single country: the United States. They only spend 13 per cent of their budget on fighting fake news in the rest of the world. Essentially, they have decided that only 13 per cent of the 166 countries using Facebook need to be addressed.

Moreover, the leakers of these documents claim something else. Even if Facebook wanted to fight hate speech, it would be entirely incapable of doing so. This is because Facebook did not have the technology to identify violence and hate speech in many languages. For example, Facebook did not have classifiers for Hindi and Bengali, which are the most widely spoken languages in India. This means that their algorithms couldn't even detect violent posts written in these languages.

Classifiers are essentially artificial language algorithms developed by Facebook and they are designed to automatically detect posts containing hate speech and calls for violence. However, it wasn't until early 2021 that Facebook developed classifier algorithms for Hindi and Bengali languages that could accurately identify and categorise incitement to violence and hatred. Even now, Facebook only has classifiers for five Indian languages, despite the platform being available in more than 20 languages in India. This makes it easier to spread violence and hate speech in those languages, with dire consequences.

Facebook admits that it lacks the technology or algorithm to block hate posts in other Indian languages and therefore, it relies on a dedicated team of 15,000 people in India to review the content of posts. However, it is questionable whether 15,000 people can effectively cover all twenty Indian languages. While Facebook claims that its team removed 8,77,000 posts containing hate speech content in India between 15 May 2021 and 31 August 2021, another problem persists.

The Facebook Papers exposed Facebook's lack of full commitment to removing all hate speech from its platform. Specifically, Facebook allows certain hate speech to persist, particularly content from Sangh Parivar organisations promoting Hindu nationalism and their supporting groups and pages. This was first reported by *The Wall Street Journal* in August 2020, and later covered by *The Times*. Facebook deems these instances as 'political sensitivities,' meaning any action against a dominant political movement could negatively impact its operations in that country. This concern over potential political repercussions leads to selective enforcement of Facebook's hate speech policies.

Furthermore, despite repeated reports, Facebook refused to remove violent posts by the Bajrang Dal. The same thing happened when a BJP member made a shocking call for violence, delivering extremely extreme hate speech against minorities and threatening to shoot people on Facebook. Some Facebook officials believed that he should be labelled as dangerous according to Facebook's rules. Facebook staff decided to permanently block this leader from Facebook, but Facebook India's head of public policy, Ankhi Das, prevented them. *The Wall Street Journal* quoted Ankhi Das as saying, 'If we punish politicians from the prime minister's party, it will destroy the business prospects of this company in India.' Ankhi Das resigned from Facebook two months after *WSJ* revealed this information. Another article by *WSJ* in December 2020 reported that Facebook's safety team considered Bajrang Dal to be advocating violence and urged labelling it as a 'dangerous organisation', with India banning the organisation. However, even Facebook did not dare to block this organisation's page or posts.

It is important to note that this is not only happening in India but also in many other countries around the world. For example, in Vietnam, the ruling party is communist, and voices of opposition against them are similarly suppressed. Facebook faces accusations of removing comments from its platform that speak against the Communist Party. The company fears that the Vietnamese government may ban Facebook from the country if it does not comply. As a result, Facebook is being forced to be complicit in many evils.

Facebook operates under the fear of losing a large market if it prioritises protecting democracy and people's lives. As a company, its primary goal is survival, making this a matter of its very existence. So, shouldn't they be forced to do these things? Why blame them so much? Isn't that what you're thinking? However, this raises another allegation.

Recently, Facebook overhauled its newsfeed algorithm. Instead of showing the latest posts, Facebook now displays the posts with the most likes and comments. The position of these posts in your newsfeed is determined based on your likes, promoting only what you like. This is not only the case with politics but also with all beliefs. Previously, when everything was timed, you would often see counter-opinions from many people. Facebook intentionally changed this system.

The truth of the matter is that without your knowledge, social media bubbles are created, and you get stuck in those bubbles that match your preferences, creating a clear polarization in society. This is explained in the Netflix documentary *Social Dilemma.* As Facebook promotes these posts more, they get more likes and comments, increasing the risk of negative breeding.

Controversial posts get more comments, and algorithms promote them more. While it is also present on YouTube to some extent, videos without much controversy or racist content get very few views. There is no doubt that people naturally gravitate towards more controversy. The next section expands on this.

QAnon Conspiracy Theory

The QAnon conspiracy theory emerged in the United States in 2017. According to this theory, the world is controlled by a secret society of Satan's servants, including Barack Obama, George Soros, Tom Hanks, and the Dalai Lama. Researchers discovered that if you liked Donald Trump's page on Facebook, the platform's algorithm would likely suggest the QAnon conspiracy theories page to you within a few days.

This is not to say that Facebook intentionally developed an algorithm to do this, but rather that the self-learning system of their artificial intelligence algorithm has learnt to nurture the darker side of human nature. They understand that people tend to repeat what they like, which leads to marked social polarisation and draws people into the web of conspiracy theories. When someone encounters these theories, they are less likely to see opposing viewpoints, as their recognition algorithm only shows them what they like. The consequences of this phenomenon are unfolding as riots in many places in the world, including the US Capitol riot, the military coup in Myanmar, and ethnic violence in Ethiopia. Many Facebook employees resigned from their jobs in frustration with this trend.

Moreover, the Facebook Papers also revealed that the platform exacerbates body image problems in girls, particularly teenagers, as they report feeling more insecure after joining the platform. Research has also shown a strong link between widespread social media use and depression, with more time spent on these platforms leading to a higher likelihood of depression.

While Facebook denies many of these allegations, they have not claimed that the internal documents are fake. Instead, they claim that they are cherry-picked reports designed to smear Facebook. However, whistleblowers maintain that this is the whole truth.

In conclusion, Facebook has been losing popularity among young people for almost ten years, with senior citizens now comprising a significant portion of the user base. This is a dramatic shift for a platform initially designed for college students. The company's researchers admit that most young people see Facebook as a platform for people between the ages of 40 and 50.

If Facebook aims to restore its former glory, it needs to address these issues and implement more regulations and improvements to the platform. The most crucial step would be to change their algorithm. Moreover, as individuals, we too should be aware of what appears in our news feed and deliberately ignore posts that promote hostility or violence against a community or certain individuals. We should also avoid letting the algorithm control our convictions and independent thinking.

You have Blood on Your Hands

In the grand epic of the Mahabharata, a tragic turn of events unfolds after the Kurukshetra war. Ashwatthama, Kritvarma, and Kripa, fuelled by a misguided sense of victory, unleashed their fury upon the sleeping warriors in the Pandava camp. The camp became engulfed in flames, and they believed they had successfully eradicated their enemies. However, their joy was short-lived when they discovered that their ally, Duryodhana, had met his demise. Ashwatthama then realised that in his rampage, he had unknowingly slaughtered the five sons of Draupadi, mistaking them for the Pandavas themselves.

Fate orchestrated a twist as the Pandavas learnt of this heinous act and got consumed by an overwhelming rage. Bhima and Arjuna, driven by an insatiable thirst for vengeance, embarked on an unwavering pursuit of Ashwatthama. Recognising the magnitude of the threat posed by the wrathful Pandavas, Ashwatthama, gripped by fear, sought refuge in the sacred ashram of the great sage, Ved Vyasa. Sensing the imminent arrival of their adversaries, the Pandavas, accompanied by the divine presence of Krishna, swiftly descended upon the ashram. The stage was set for a climactic confrontation.

In a moment, Bhima, with his immense strength, struck out at Ashwatthama, determined to bring him to his knees. Sensing the impending danger, Ashwatthama, driven by desperation, unleashed the formidable power of the *brahmastra*, a cataclysmic weapon, towards the Pandavas. In a retaliatory move, Arjuna, a master archer, released his own brahmastra, directing it towards Ashwatthama. The clash of these mighty weapons threatened to unleash unimaginable devastation upon the world. In a display of divine intervention, Ved Vyasa, the sage of profound wisdom, stepped forward and intercepted the airborne brahmastras, suspending them in mid-air. Krishna, the all-knowing and wise guide, comprehended the catastrophic consequences that would result from the collision of these unstoppable forces and commanded both Arjuna and Ashwatthama to retract their weapons, urging them to prevent the impending catastrophe. Arjuna, obedient to Krishna's command, successfully withdrew his brahmastra, diffusing the tension. However, Ashwatthama, plagued by ignorance, confessed that he possessed no knowledge of how to retract the unleashed weapon.

In the modern world, we are witnessing a similar event. Facebook, initially created as an online photo-sharing platform for university students, has grown into a global behemoth. Its founder, Mark Zuckerberg, stood before the US Senate, much like Ashwatthama after unleashing the deadly brahmastra. During a crucial US Senate hearing, Mark Zuckerberg, the visionary leader of Facebook, surprised attendees with a heartfelt apology to parents whose children have suffered due to the company's online platforms. This powerful moment unfolded amidst accusations that Zuckerberg had inadvertently created a 'product that's killing people'. Addressing the families present at the hearing, some of whom held up photographs of their affected children, Zuckerberg expressed his remorse, saying, 'I am sorry for everything you have all been through. No one should endure the hardships that your families have suffered.'

The hearing, titled 'Big Tech and the Online Child Sexual Exploitation Crisis,' brought together prominent technology executives, including TikTok CEO Shou Zi Chew, Snapchat co-founder Evan Spiegel, Discord CEO Jason Citron, and Linda Yaccarino, the head of online platform X (formerly Twitter). Senator Dick Durbin, the chair of the committee and US Senate Majority Whip, emphasised in his opening remarks that technology companies bear responsibility for the dangers children face online. He criticised their design choices, insufficient investment in trust and safety measures, and prioritisation of engagement and profits over basic security. Senator Lindsey Graham took a particularly strong stance, accusing Zuckerberg of having blood on his hands and asserting that Facebook's product was causing harm. In response, Zuckerberg acknowledged the challenges of keeping young people safe online and emphasised the need for evolving defences as criminals adapt their tactics. He also highlighted research indicating that, overall, social media does not have a detrimental impact on young people's mental health. Despite the criticism from the US Senate, the world points fingers at the tech industry, those who unscrupulously wield digital weapons.

The Infamous Cambridge Analytica

Many people freely share things on Facebook and Instagram that they wouldn't share even with their closest friends. The cyber world gives them a false sense of security, thinking that no one will search for or harass them there. This false sense of security is known as the 'online disinhibition effect'. Unfortunately, we still haven't fully grasped the danger of this phenomenon. Cambridge Analytica was one of the first to make us realise that there are few people more dangerous than lone criminals with malicious intentions.

But what exactly is Cambridge Analytica? Today, it is just a non-functioning political consulting firm, but its actions have raised serious concerns in the tech world. Let's take a look at how Cambridge Analytica operated in the cyber world:

1. **Data Collection**

   Cambridge Analytica obtained personal information from millions of Facebook users without their consent. They used a personality quiz app called 'This Is Your Digital Life' to collect this data not only from quiz takers but also from their Facebook friends.

2. **Psychometric Profiling**

   Using the collected data, Cambridge Analytica created psychometric profiles of individuals. These profiles were based on personality traits, political beliefs, and other psychological factors. They then used this information to send targeted political messages tailored to each individual's beliefs and interests.

3. **Micro-targeting**

   Cambridge Analytica employed micro-targeting techniques based on the psychometric profiles. They categorised individuals into specific groups and delivered highly persuasive and emotionally resonant political content to each group.

4. **Influence Campaigns**

It was later revealed that Cambridge Analytica had been involved in various political campaigns worldwide, including the 2016 US presidential election and the UK's Brexit referendum. They strategically designed messages to evoke emotional responses and reinforce existing beliefs, using their psychometric profiling and micro-targeting methods to influence people.

5. **Dark Ads**

Dark ads refer to political ads specifically targeted at certain groups but disguised to look like regular news stories in users' feeds. Many people fell for these ads without realising they were part of a political campaign.

By implementing these strategies, Cambridge Analytica attempted to manipulate the world order by exploiting Facebook's data-sharing policies. It is unlikely that Cambridge Analytica was a one-time incident; there may be more similar incidents in the future. Although there are laws in place to prevent the collection and misuse of personal information for political purposes, the world often prioritises profit over these regulations. Corporations and governments are driven by the desire for profit, and this can lead to unethical practices.

The Transition

Facebook, which began as a photo-sharing app for college students, has undergone seismic transformations. Initially launched at Harvard University in 2003 as Facemash, it allowed students to judge their peers' attractiveness. However, it was shut down after two days due to violations of university policy by its creator, Mark Zuckerberg. Despite name changes and evolving policies, agendas, ethics, and motives, Facebook's growth and adaptation have persisted.

As of April 2024, Meta—the parent company of Facebook, Instagram, WhatsApp, and Messenger—reported 3.24 billion daily active users across its platforms, marking a 7 per cent year-over-year increase. In Q4 2023, Meta revealed that 3.98 billion people used at least one of its core products monthly, surpassing most countries' populations.

The transition from a fun college app to the tech behemoth Meta has driven the company to prioritise profit, align with questionable interests, and often ignore inhumane global events. However, abstaining from these platforms altogether is not the solution. Instead, prioritising safety and exercising prudence and wisdom while utilising these digital tools is crucial. Ultimately, the responsibility rests in our hands to navigate the digital landscape with caution and mindfulness.

The Rise of the Digital Oligopoly

An oligopoly is a market structure dominated by a small number of firms. Unlike monopolies where one firm controls the entire market, or perfect competition with numerous small firms, oligopolies consist of just a few companies with significant market power. This concentration allows them to influence prices and other market outcomes.

Over the past decade, a few multinational corporations that began as friendly start-ups have evolved into an oligopoly known as GAFAM (Google, Apple, Facebook, Amazon, and Microsoft). This group controls vast digital territories through immense market power and financial clout. Their dominance is reinforced by intellectual and industrial property rights, sometimes leading to patent wars. This trend represents internet privatisation, transforming it into a concentrated resource pool in what Ugo Pagano terms 'intellectual monopoly capitalism.'

As the internet evolves, the influence of these tech giants raises critical questions about digital democracy's future and equitable resource distribution in our increasingly connected world.

The Promise and Perils of Digital Technologies

Initially celebrated as a democratic, participatory, and decentralised platform, especially with Web 2.0's rise enabling user-generated content and social media interactions, the internet's early optimism has given way to a more sobering reality. Today, the internet serves as a battleground where various social groups, political institutions, and multinational corporations vie for influence and control. Digital communication channels have become arenas for power struggles, reflecting a complex interplay of often antagonistic economic and political interests. This evolution demonstrates that the internet's structure and use are shaped more by these powerful forces than by any inherent democratic nature.

Digital networking technologies have become integral to daily life over the last decade. Our social interactions, work, entertainment, and education are all facilitated by electronic devices and online services. While offering unprecedented convenience, these technologies have permeated every aspect of our personal, professional, and public spheres, often without our conscious awareness. This pervasive digital colonisation has unfolded within a globalised, deregulated economy that tends to concentrate resources and power in a few hands which has led to significant challenges. Companies like Google, Facebook, and Amazon wield immense control over what we see, how we interact, and how our data is used. This concentration has implications for privacy, security, and the nature of democratic discourse.

For instance, Facebook excels in utilising information users willingly share, such as personal data and social connections. This data allows Facebook to offer highly targeted advertising tools without solely relying on tracking devices like cookies. Moreover, mobile applications, particularly those developed or acquired by Facebook, are user information goldmines. Apps like Instagram and WhatsApp provide detailed insights into users' daily activities, preferences, and social interactions. Facebook can track the types of posts users engage with, products they search for and purchase, and locations they frequent. This data is invaluable for creating highly targeted advertising campaigns more likely to resonate with users.

Beyond app usage data, Facebook's Instant Messenger plays a significant role in data collection. The app can monitor links exchanged in messages, providing further insights into users' interests and online behaviour. Additionally, concerns and reports have arisen about apps using smartphone microphones to capture ambient sounds, which can be analysed to infer user activities and preferences. Although Facebook has denied using microphones for ad targeting, the potential for such data collection exists, raising privacy concerns among users.

Such advanced tracking methods and strategic use of user data by tech giants have created a powerful, lucrative data market. These companies leverage extensive user information to enhance targeted advertising, maintaining dominance through strategic partnerships and innovative advertising models.

Stealth Data Collection and Manipulation by Tech Companies

The ability of tech companies like Facebook to collect data stealthily and manipulate user experiences based on this data is a growing concern. Stealth data collection involves gathering information about users without their explicit knowledge or consent. This can occur through various means, such as cookies, device fingerprinting, and tracking pixels embedded in web pages and emails.

Tech companies use this data to create detailed user profiles, which are then used to deliver highly personalised content and advertisements. While this can enhance user experience by providing relevant information and ads, it also raises significant privacy issues. Users may be unaware of the extent of data being collected or how it is being used, leading to a lack of transparency and control over personal information.

Facebook's central role on smartphones and its extensive data collection capabilities underscore the broader issue of stealth data collection and manipulation by tech companies. While these practices enable highly targeted and effective advertising, they also raise important questions about user privacy and consent. As tech companies continue to innovate and find new ways to collect and leverage data, it is crucial for users to be aware of these practices and for regulators to ensure adequate protections are in place to safeguard user privacy. The balance between innovation and privacy will be key to maintaining user trust and the long-term sustainability of the digital advertising ecosystem.

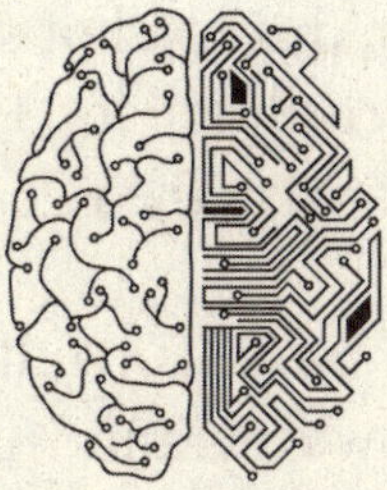

Chapter 12

Digital Tribalism

A Need for Acceptance

Let's examine psychologist Professor Abraham Maslow's renowned 'hierarchy of needs'. Maslow's pyramid consists of five levels. From the bottom, human needs are as follows: physiological (food and clothing), safety (job security), love and belonging (friendship), self-esteem and esteem from others, and the ultimate state of self-actualisation at the top.

Professor Maslow asserts that once the basic survival needs in this pyramid are met, such as food, water, shelter, clothing, warmth, sex, and sleep, higher-level needs begin to motivate our behaviour. These include social needs like relatedness, mutual cooperation, group belonging, self-esteem, prestige, achievement, mastery, independence, and the desire for fame, respect, or status.

As per a report, most people spend 40 per cent of their time talking about themselves or their feelings. However, in online communication, this level of self-disclosure increases to 80 per cent. According to Harvard neuroscientist Dr Diana Tamir, this triggers the release of dopamine, giving people pleasure.

In the cyber world, you can fulfil all the needs at the highest level of Maslow's pyramid in one way or another. Online anonymity provides a sense of security. Joining an online community or participating in a multiplayer online game offers a sense of self-worth. When your Instagram photos or Facebook posts receive likes, your longing for recognition is satisfied. When you post information about yourself online and others see and like it, you feel accepted, acknowledged, and heard. The joy it brings is substantial.

The internet offers a unique environment where individuals can meet psychological needs that may prove challenging in the physical realm. Social media platforms, forums, and online communities provide spaces for free self-expression and the validation of others. The instant gratification from online interactions can be incredibly satisfying, reinforcing the behaviour and encouraging continued use.

However, this digital fulfilment carries a downside. The constant need for validation can lead to excessive screen time, impacting real-world relationships and responsibilities. It can also foster an unhealthy dependence on virtual interactions for self-worth, which may not translate into real-life confidence and fulfilment. Additionally, the anonymity providing security can enable negative behaviours like cyberbullying and harassment, harming others and disrupting the sense of community.

While the cyber world offers myriad opportunities to fulfil higher psychological needs, balancing online interactions with real-world experiences is essential. Awareness of the potential pitfalls can help individuals harness the internet to enhance well-being without compromising mental health or real-life relationships. By understanding and moderating our online behaviour, we can capitalise on the positive aspects of digital interactions while minimising negative impacts, leading to a more balanced, fulfilling life online and off.

The Seeking System: The Science of Our Online Habits

Searching for information, shopping online, or reconnecting with old classmates on Facebook can be enjoyable activities. To explore this further, let's consider an interesting experiment conducted by Jack Panksepp, a neuroscientist at Washington State University.

Professor Panksepp conducts laboratory experiments on rats. He found that living beings possess an innate mechanism called the 'seeking system'. This process of search drives humans and animals to seek information that will aid their survival. It produces dopamine in the organism, and as a result, the search process becomes pleasurable. He states, 'This "seeking system" is the motivational mechanism that drives mammals out of their beds, dens, and burrows every day.' Dr Mary Temple Grandin, a renowned scientist from the University of Colorado, has extensively researched this topic. She found that the act of searching is highly stimulating. Her studies revealed that allowing caged animals to hunt or search for food, rather than being fed directly, provides them with more pleasure and extends their lifespan.

Professionals like cops, detectives, investigative journalists, and research scientists often experience the joy of investigating and exploring. Before the advent of the internet, they were among the few who could truly savour the excitement and rewards of quest and discovery. The human urge to seek and explore has fueled and nourished us for centuries. Dr Jack Panksepp, a neuroscientist at Washington State University, was the first to provide a biochemical explanation for this phenomenon. He discovered that dopamine, produced during searching and foraging, stimulates and pleases the brain, likely enabling humankind to adapt so well to new environments. This exploration grants us a psychological reward, and it is the same reward system that keeps us searching online.

Cyberspace is akin to outer space when it comes to searching. It is infinite, vast, and boundless. Online searching provides us with a smaller version of the same pleasure we derive from alcohol and drugs. It continually amazes us with breaking news, statistics, personal messages, and entertainment. Alerts, notifications, lights, beeps, and other visual triggers from new apps, ads, games, and social networking sites all create a signal in the human brain equivalent to primitive mating.

In essence, the innate 'seeking system' identified by Professor Panksepp explains why the act of searching and discovering—whether in the wild, through professional investigations, or online—feels so innately rewarding. The biochemical reactions in our brains, particularly the release of dopamine, render the act of seeking not merely essential for survival but inherently pleasurable. This pleasure drives us to continue exploring, learning, and connecting in ever-evolving ways. As we navigate the boundless realms of cyberspace, remaining mindful of how we wield these digital tools is paramount. By understanding the science underpinning our search behaviours, we can harness this knowledge to enhance our experiences while ensuring responsible and wise technology utilisation.

Digital Tribalism

The Latin term 'addictus' was initially used to describe the period an indentured slave had to serve their master, implying a state of slavery. Slavery, in turn, was also referred to as 'addiction'. Nowadays, we can observe this addictive behaviour in many people around us. For instance, when you go out for lunch and chat with a friend, but they seem distracted, frequently checking their phone. Is your friend intentionally being rude? Of course not. They undoubtedly value their real-world relationship with you. However, the sad reality is that the pleasure they derive from talking to you in person is overshadowed by the pleasure they get from checking their phone's notifications. None of the WhatsApp messages your friend receives are urgent, and you both know their phone won't deliver a life-and-death scenario message. Nevertheless, your friend can't resist the urge to check every notification.

The irresistible pull of mobile phones can be explained by a psychological phenomenon known as signalling theory. Originally developed in the study of animal behaviour, signalling theory explores communication between individuals, including sexual selection based on signals emitted by females during mate selection. Animals use various signals, such as sight, sound, smell, chemicals, and touch, to communicate and attract each other. For example, hens prefer to mate with roosters with the largest tails, and male peacocks with the most peals attract more mates. Signalling theory also helps evolutionary psychologists understand human interactions and the cues of attention and choices in these interactions.

From an evolutionary lens, our brains react intensely to these digital signals akin to our instinctive responses to snakes and spiders—due to their historical unpredictability and threat. Each phone alert triggers a response as urgent as encountering potential peril in the wild. Phone manufacturers and marketers exploit this innate response, leveraging signalling cues—like Apple's iconic white earbuds—to foster a sense of belonging and superiority within consumer tribes.

Looking ahead, integrating new sensory signals like scents or vibrations could further amplify mobile devices' allure. This evolution raises concerns over digital addiction's tightening grip and its toll on personal relationships and well-being. As we navigate this digital terrain, understanding the psychological underpinnings driving our behaviours is crucial. Balancing our technological reliance with mindful engagement in real-world interactions will be key to preserving meaningful connections and individual autonomy amidst the age of digital tribalism.

Digital Desires: The Impact of Online Sexual Content

Cyberspace proves highly fertile ground for sexual and erotic content. The quest for explicit material and the human desire to view naked people engaged in sexual activity have flourished over the past two decades. Porn sites could even be deemed the internet's backbone, garnering more visitors than Netflix, Amazon, and Twitter combined—representing 30 per cent of the total internet industry. In 2015, the mobile phone pornography business was estimated at a staggering $15 billion value.

The internet has provided unparalleled access to sexual content, making it easier for individuals to explore their desires. Pornography, in particular, has become a significant part of the online experience for many. With its immense popularity, the porn industry has grown into a major economic force, with adult content websites consistently ranking among the internet's most visited.

According to T*he American Journal of Drug and Alcohol Abuse,* many men and women struggle with cybersex addiction. Therapists report an increasing number of patients addicted to online sex, and such individuals may suffer severe trauma, depression, anxiety, and excessive addiction. The experience often begins as a brief curiosity but can quickly escalate in frequency and intensity.

Consider the following case: Dr Mary Ann Layden, a psychologist at the University of Pennsylvania, recounts a young man so addicted to internet pornography that he couldn't attend a job interview, unable to step away from his computer. Brain scans of such individuals reveal patterns of change akin to other drug addicts. These changes indicate the brain's reward system is activated similarly by pornography and drugs, reinforcing addictive behaviours and making breaking free from habits immensely challenging.

Ethical Dimensions of Online Sexual Content

The widespread availability and consumption of online sexual content raise several societal and ethical concerns. Issues such as the objectification of individuals, especially women, the normalization of certain sexual behaviours, and the potential impact on relationships and personal well-being are areas of ongoing debate. Additionally, the accessibility of such content to minors poses significant risks, necessitating discussions around regulation and parental controls.

When exploring the intriguing realm of online sexual content, it is critical to recognise its profound and multifaceted impact. This digital domain not only caters to diverse desires and plays a significant economic role in the internet industry but also presents a range of psychological, social, and ethical challenges. The rise of cybersex and pornography addiction is a pressing issue that parallels other forms of addictive behaviours, necessitating attention from mental health professionals and society.

Comprehending the influence of online sexual content is paramount in addressing its effects and promoting responsible, healthy digital usage. As we navigate the vast digital age landscape, adopting a balanced approach that acknowledges both the benefits and potential risks found within cyberspace's erotic frontier is crucial. By cultivating awareness and understanding, we can ensure individuals engage with digital tools respectfully, fostering positive online experiences while safeguarding well-being.

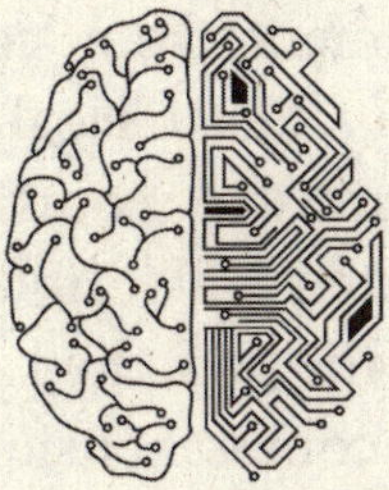

Chapter 13

Digital Apps and Children's Cognitive Development

The Impact of Digital Apps

The proliferation of digital apps has fundamentally reshaped the landscape of childhood, offering new avenues for learning, entertainment, and socialisation. However, this digital revolution also raises concerns about its impact on children's developing brains. Understanding both the potential benefits and risks is crucial for parents, educators, and policymakers. In this chapter, we will explore this topic in detail.

Beyond Screens: The Importance of Human Interaction for Babies

In 1997, Julie Aigner Clark and her husband William Clark created *Baby Einstein*, a video series designed for children under two featuring toys, cartoons, sounds, music, stories, numbers, and words in various languages. It swiftly became a successful franchise earning a whopping $25 million yearly, even attracting investment from companies like Disney. However, *Baby Einstein* faced legal issues over time due to false advertising claims. A court investigation revealed valid concerns supported by various studies. Researchers discovered children who watched *Baby Einstein* videos showed no better word comprehension than those who spent screen-free time with their parents. Another study suggested these videos might even delay speech development in infants aged eight to sixteen months.

Understanding these dynamics is paramount as we navigate childhood development's intricate realm in our increasingly digital world. Today, a prevailing belief holds that electronic devices enhance a child's cognitive abilities from an early age. However, medical insights shed a different light.

Contrary to popular belief, excessive screen and digital stimulation exposure can impede–rather than facilitate–baby brain development. Babies are innately inclined towards human-face interaction, particularly of their caregivers. They remarkably recognise faces and derive joy from gazing at other babies' faces, akin to adults. Moreover, immense pleasure and stimulation come from focusing on their mother's face and eye contact which is crucial for mental development and world understanding. No animation app, digital avatar, or 3D cartoon can replicate or replace this vital human interaction's profound impact. It is within the genuine caregiver connection that a baby's cognitive and emotional development thrives, far surpassing any digital substitute's capabilities.

The Secret Lives of Teens Online

In today's digital world, children and teens are increasingly seeking privacy as they navigate their online activities and social interactions. This quest for privacy is particularly evident among teenagers in India, where smartphones and gaming consoles are highly valued. Globally, a significant majority of young people (59 per cent) engage in behaviours such as clearing browser histories and concealing details about their online activities.

Recent studies underscore the extent to which teens go to keep their online lives hidden from their parents. A staggering 69 per cent of teenagers admit to actively hiding their online activities. This trend reflects a desire among adolescents to carve out their own identities and spaces away from adult supervision.

Navigating Teen Privacy in the Digital Age

The prevalence of secrecy among teens raises important considerations for parents, educators, and policymakers alike. While privacy is a natural part of adolescence, it also presents challenges in terms of parental oversight and guidance. Understanding the motivations behind teens' online behaviours—whether for personal exploration, social interaction, or protection of privacy—is crucial for fostering healthy digital habits.

As children and teens continue to shape their identities and navigate the complexities of the online world, the need for balanced approaches to privacy and supervision becomes increasingly apparent. While respecting adolescents' autonomy and privacy rights, it is essential for adults to maintain open communication channels and provide guidance on safe and responsible internet use. By fostering a supportive environment that balances privacy with parental oversight, we can help teens develop the digital skills and resilience needed to thrive in today's interconnected world.

Nurturing Healthy Digital Habits in Children

Establishing a strong bond with your children is crucial for effective and beneficial discipline. Spending quality time with them during their formative years and showing genuine interest in their activities are important demonstrations of care. It is vital to avoid excessive phone use during these times and show happiness can be found beyond mobile devices like cell phones, tablets, iPads, online games, and the internet.

Teaching children wise and transparent mobile phone use is crucial. Holding them accountable for gadget use and utilising monitoring apps can be helpful. Adhering to age restrictions for internet and mobile device access, and seeking child expert guidance before purchasing children's gadgets, can also prove beneficial.

Experts do not recommend giving mobile devices to children under six, and screen time should be limited to 30 minutes or less for young children and under an hour for older kids. Establishing guidelines, limits, and rules for gadget use can ensure their safety. While children may sometimes test parent-set boundaries, sticking to originally agreed timeframes instils trust and security. Predefined rewards and consequences can also effectively help children understand responsible gadget use importance, with incentives encouraging healthy behaviour and consequences discouraging misuse.

Some countries have commendably regulated children's electronic device use. Taiwan recently introduced legislation making parents responsible for misuse's negative effects. Similar recommendations and guidelines exist in Canada and Australia. However, no specific restrictions are in place in India or America.

Parents should also take the initiative to check which apps and games are suitable for children, providing pre-approved websites, apps, and resources. Learning to use parental controls offered by browsers and devices can help prevent exposure to harmful content. Teaching children to protect their online identity is crucial. Emphasise the importance of not sharing personal information on sites and apps. Encourage a 'think before you post' policy and teach proper online etiquette to guide them in making responsible choices. It is essential to educate children about the permanence of online information and the potential risks associated with disclosing personal details.

Setting a positive example is vital. Limit phone usage at home, avoid sharing sensitive pictures and videos of children, and be mindful of the family's digital footprint—all contribute to creating a healthy digital environment. Establish designated gadget-free times, such as during meals or before bedtime, to prevent over-reliance on devices. Spend quality time as a family without distractions to foster deeper connections and reinforce the value of offline interactions.

Having access to your child's social media accounts and monitoring their online activity until adulthood can help ensure their safety. Get to know their online friends and discourage connections with strangers. By being present and engaged, parents can deter potential abusers and protect their children from harm. It is also important to recognise that effective communication is key. Rather than solely focusing on correcting children, engage in open discussions about potential cyber world problems they may encounter. Trust that their sense of digital security will naturally develop over time.

Nurturing healthy digital habits in children requires a mindful approach. Prioritise genuine human interaction, set limits on screen time, teach responsible gadget use, and maintain open communication to ensure their well-being in the digital era. By implementing these strategies, we can empower children to navigate the digital landscape safely and develop a healthy balance between technology and real-life experiences.

Here is a concise summary of all the essential principles covered above.

- Your baby's tiny brain is fast-growing. They develop through sensory stimulation. Therefore, consciously consider the development of all the senses. A baby's early interactions and experiences are encoded in the brain and remain forever.
- Don't use a digital babysitter or future robot nanny to look after your beloved baby. Toddlers and children need closeness to real people. There is no substitute for a real human being.
- Wait until the age of two or three before giving your child screen time. Consciously limit screen time for your child, considering how screens may influence how they develop.
- Realise that babies are naturally empathetic and will have a hard time dealing with things that are emotionally hurtful, distressing, or violent.
- Pay attention to the content of the videos they watch. Look at how long the television is on, whether your kids are watching or not.

- Consciously monitor how often you check your mobile phone and try to limit unnecessary usage. Be the role model you want your child to emulate.
- Don't be fooled by marketing claims. Science shows us that tablet apps are not as good for education as they claim. In fact, screen time can cause developmental delays in children. Additionally, it can cause attention problems and language development disorders in children.
- Spend quality time with your children, limiting phone usage during these moments to prioritise genuine human interaction.
- Teach children responsible and transparent gadget usage, utilising monitoring apps and age-appropriate restrictions.
- Establish clear guidelines and reasonable limits on screen time, with a system of rewards and consequences to encourage responsible use.
- Stay informed about relevant legislation and expert recommendations regarding children's electronic device usage.
- Carefully review and pre-approve apps, games, and websites before allowing children access, providing guidance on online safety.
- Lead by example: limit your own phone usage, avoid sharing sensitive content involving children, and designate gadget-free times for the family.
- Monitor and provide guidance on your children's social media activity until they reach adulthood, fostering open communication about potential online risks.

- Rather than solely correcting children, engage in open discussions about cyber world challenges to gradually build their sense of digital security over time.

Embracing Boredom: Fostering Creativity and Resilience in Children

In every society, there is a prevailing belief that people should always be engaged in some activity, adhering to an unspoken rule of constant busyness. This issue is particularly relevant for children, who are naturally full of energy and eager to engage in various activities. When idle moments arise, boredom sets in—a concept they are not yet equipped to understand. Unfortunately, many parents also struggle to comprehend and manage boredom. Whenever their child feels bored, parents often rush to fill this void with activities like phone games, television, or music.

This constant attempt to eliminate idleness can lead to overstimulation and prevents children from learning the valuable skill of taking a pause and appreciating life. Simply avoiding overstimulation and busyness is not enough; we must address the root cause and understand boredom itself. Let's explore what modern psychological research reveals about boredom and its impact on development.

Dr Sandy Mann of the University of Lancashire and Dr Sandi Mann of the University of East Anglia conducted a study along with Teresa Belten and others. They found that creative and innovative thoughts, ideas, and actions are more common in children who engage in relatively boring and repetitive activities. Another study published by the University of Texas in the United States in 2013 states that boredom, loneliness, and idleness help divert our mental energy to more productive, useful, and imaginative pursuits.

The University of California conducted a study on this topic and uncovered the following findings: 'Wandering minds are not always signs of laziness. They often increase our mental energy and nurture our inner ability to analyse problems holistically and find solutions. Boredom is not always a problem.'

Advantages of Embracing Boredom

Contrary to popular belief, boredom plays a crucial role in child development and overall mental health. Let's look at some of the key practical benefits it can offer.

1. Boredom can teach about happiness

Boredom teaches children that happiness and joy aren't always found externally, a valuable lesson in their growth. Childhood, a period of rapid development, can benefit from less screen time. Encourage them to observe the world—people, animals, objects—and understand actions and expressions. This fosters independent thinking and mental resilience. Without learning to tolerate boredom, children may grow impatient and overly reliant on external stimulation.

2. Boredom can enhance creativity

Studies have shown that there is a strong connection between daydreaming and imagination. Boredom prompts our minds to wander, unleashing our imaginations. This mental muscle strengthens with practice, akin to exercising a muscle. Embracing boredom can thus cultivate our imagination over time.

3. Boredom can reduce stress

One of the lesser-known benefits of boredom is its ability to reduce stress. When children are constantly engaged with screens and activities, their brains remain in a perpetual state of stimulation. This constant stimulation can lead to mental fatigue and increased stress levels. In contrast, allowing children to experience periods of boredom gives their brains a chance to rest and reset. Boredom encourages them to find alternative sources of entertainment and fulfilment that are not reliant on digital devices.

4. Embracing Boredom for Health and Well-Being

Encouraging children to embrace boredom as a natural part of life can foster resilience and creativity. By providing opportunities for unstructured play, outdoor activities, and hobbies that do not involve screens, parents and caregivers help children develop a healthy relationship with technology. Balancing screen time with periods of boredom allows children to recharge mentally and physically, promoting overall well-being.

In our fast-paced digital world, understanding the importance of boredom is crucial for promoting children's health and development. Boredom provides valuable opportunities for self-reflection, creativity, and stress reduction. By encouraging unstructured activities and limiting screen time, we support children's physical, emotional, and cognitive growth. Embracing boredom as a natural and beneficial aspect of life helps cultivate resilience, creativity, and a balanced approach to technology—benefits that extend beyond childhood into adulthood.

Chapter 14

The Perilous Promise of AI

Science, undoubtedly, holds immense value in understanding and explaining the world around us. It has provided us with remarkable insights and technological marvels. But when science becomes a religion, when we overly rely on its methods and principles, we fall into the trap of scientism. This rigid belief disregards anything that cannot be studied or explained through scientific means, dismissing it as invalid or inconsequential. However, it is crucial to recognise that the absence of evidence is not evidence of absence. To be an informed citizen, one must possess a scientific temper while also acknowledging the limitations of scientific exploration. Technology, a byproduct of science, is like a double-edged sword, capable of both great good and immense harm.

In today's world, the advancements in artificial intelligence (AI) have reached unprecedented levels. However, as with any powerful tool, there is a lurking danger that must not be ignored. Just as the sword of Damocles hung precariously above his head, AI poses a similar threat to humanity.

One significant concern surrounding AI is the impact it will have on jobs. AI is being utilised in various fields such as marketing, manufacturing, and healthcare. It is projected that between 2020 and 2025, approximately 85 million jobs will be lost due to AI, posing a significant challenge. And though AI is expected to create around 97 million new jobs by 2025, there is another issue to contend with. Many workers may lack the necessary skills for these new roles. Even highly educated professionals such as lawyers, accountants, and doctors may find themselves at risk of job displacement due to AI's capability to handle complex legal processes and efficiently process vast amounts of information.

Another area of concern is the use of AI to manipulate people on social media. A 2018 report highlighted this as a significant problem. We are already witnessing the impact of politicians utilising social media platforms to spread their ideas. The emergence of deepfakes has further complicated matters, particularly in the realms of politics and society. This technology enables the dissemination of misinformation and even threats of war. It has become increasingly challenging to discern truth from the lies presented before our eyes. Trusting our own senses has become a confusing endeavour as deepfakes undermine our ability to rely on what we see and hear. Thus, as we celebrate the remarkable progress in AI and other technological advancements, it is our collective responsibility to ensure their responsible deployment. We must tread cautiously, considering the potential consequences for future generations.

In this chapter, we will explore the potential dangers of AI, gain insights from industry experts, and propose ways to responsibly navigate this new paradigm.

21st-Century Big Brother

With the advent of artificial intelligence, privacy has become a myth. AI can meticulously monitor citizens' activities, locations, and communications, including their preferences and even personal interests. AI can be used to identify and target individuals critical of, or perceived as a threat to, the government. Moreover, fascist regimes can leverage such extensive surveillance data to intimidate, arrest, or detain individuals expressing dissenting views.

By collecting and analysing data from various sources like Facebook, Google, Microsoft, Apple, Uber, Zomato, and smartwatches, governments gain valuable insights into citizens' beliefs and opinions. AI-powered bots and automated accounts can flood social media platforms with fake news, divisive content, and misinformation, causing confusion and exacerbating societal tensions. Additionally, AI algorithms have the capability to analyse individuals' online behaviour to identify disabilities, illnesses, fears, and biases. This information can be used by governments and corporations to develop highly personalised strategies of manipulation and deception.

Facial recognition technology, powered by AI, enables the identification and tracking of individuals in public spaces. Governments can exploit this technology to target activists and dissidents, compromising their anonymity and security. AI can also be utilised to clone voices, creating convincing deepfake audio recordings that can be used to impersonate political figures and spread false information.

It is important to note here that when institutions or governments possess comprehensive information about individuals, they can easily decide whether to nurture or weaken them. AI can be employed to reinforce totalitarian governments, presenting a facade of efficient systems and isolated incidents. This allows them to create a constant battle against an enemy, instilling fear and horror in people's minds. Artificial Intelligence has become a powerful tool for manipulating and controlling public perception.

In China, facial recognition technology is now being used on cameras installed in offices, schools, and public spaces. This enables governments to track people's movements and know their activities, associations, and beliefs. In the United States, law enforcement agencies employ computer programs that attempt to predict crime hotspots. However, these programs have faced substantial criticism for their inherent biases, particularly in unfairly targeting black individuals.

Risks and Concerns of AI

As AI technology advances, its influence on society becomes increasingly significant and multifaceted. Let's look at some of the negative issues related to AI.

1. **A Biased AI World**

   AI can exhibit biases in various domains, including gender and race, as noted by Olga Russakovsky, a computer science professor at Princeton University. Since AI is created by humans, it inherently reflects their biases. In some cases, these biases may be even more pronounced due to limited exposure and understanding of diverse groups among AI researchers. This can result in AI struggling to comprehend people from different cultures. To mitigate these issues, those involved in developing AI must exercise greater caution and ensure that their biases do not harm minority groups.

2. AI Exacerbates Inequality

AI has been shown to exacerbate the wealth gap. For instance, if AI is used in job selection, its inherent biases may lead to talented individuals being rejected based on language, appearance, or race. Therefore, as machines replace human workers, the wages of ordinary people can be reduced by up to 70 per cent. While some individuals who primarily work in office settings may view this technology as a boon, it is crucial to consider its impact on people in other fields. Merely assuming that AI will create more jobs or benefit everyone ignores the potential harm it can cause to certain groups. We must thoughtfully assess how AI can be beneficial to some while avoiding harm to others.

3. A World Without Morality

AI concerns not only technologists, media reporters, and politicians, but also religious leaders. In 2019, Pope Francis expressed his worries about global peace in the face of AI being used to spread false ideas and disinformation. He emphasised the need for careful control and regulation of AI development and its operations. Some AI tools, like ChatGPT, are already causing significant issues in schools and stifling creativity in children. Many also fear that corporations' profit-driven motives may lead to unethical use of AI.

4. AI Weapons

Technologists and activists are raising alarm about autonomous weapons powered by artificial intelligence. It is widely known that many countries employ technology for military purposes. There is already a race among nations to develop such intelligent weaponry. This trend poses a grave threat to humanity itself, as the consequences of these weapons falling into the wrong hands could be catastrophic. Countries must ensure that AI is not misused for destructive purposes, but the question remains: who can provide such assurance?

5. Totalitarian Tendencies of AI

Governments that disregard democratic values may utilise AI to manipulate their citizens in various ways. AI can be employed to generate deepfake videos, synthesised speech, or false articles with the aim of spreading misinformation. Authoritarian governments may exploit this technique to shape public opinion and suppress dissent.

Internet of Things

The Internet of Things (IoT) refers to the interconnection of electronic devices through sensors, software, and the internet. While it offers convenience in tasks like opening doors, controlling heaters, or turning off lights, it comes at a price.

IoT devices extensively collect sensitive user information without clear knowledge of how it is used, stored, and shared. The concept of privacy becomes virtually non-existent for IoT users. For instance, smartwatches are equipped with a variety of sensors, including accelerometers, gyroscopes, heart rate monitors, GPS, ambient light sensors, barometers, SpO2 sensors, EDA sensors, NFC, compasses, and pedometers. These sensors collect extensive biometric data, such as heart rate, sleep patterns, physical activity, blood pressure, conversations, messages, and browsing history.

This data is highly valuable and generates significant income, yet even the government often remains unaware of who has access to it.

Professor Yuval Noah Harari, a renowned writer, highlights that smartwatches primarily transmit information to insurance companies. They constantly monitor activity and analyse basic physical conditions, giving insurers the ability to deny claims or increase premiums based on this data. Harari further warns about wearable biometrics, such as neural lace implants, which have the potential to monitor emotions and thoughts. This opens the door for profit-driven corporations or authoritarian regimes to manipulate people's emotions and control their actions.

Corporations and governments often justify surveillance as a means to reduce crime, ensure social security, and protect public health. However, in this pursuit of the 'common good,' there is a serious risk of violating human rights. Thus, it is important to be cautious and mindful of the AI assistants we use, such as Alexa, Siri, Google Assistant, Android/Apple TV, smartphones, computers, surround cameras, and smartwatches. These devices have the capability to record conversations and gather information, potentially transforming us into mere machines or cyber aliens. Therefore, it is crucial to use these gadgets with care and wisdom to prevent any unwanted intrusions.

Shaping the Future: Balancing Technological Progress and Human Well-being

History has shown us the perils of unchecked technological advancements. Albert Einstein's groundbreaking discovery that matter can be converted into energy ultimately led to the creation of devastating weapons like the atomic bomb and hydrogen bomb. Dr J. Robert Oppenheimer, the father of the atomic bomb, himself lamented the consequences of his own invention, realising the irreversible change it brought upon the world. Even today, experts in the field of AI estimate a significant chance that this technology could potentially bring about the destruction of humanity. Similarly, 50 per cent of AI researchers today believe there is a 10 per cent chance or more of humans going extinct due to an inability to manage advanced AI. This warning is timely, given that Tristan Harris and Aza Raskin, co-founders of the Center for Humane Technology, are building awareness of technology's negative impact on society. As seen in their Emmy-winning Netflix documentary, *The Social Dilemma,* which reached 100 million viewers across 190 nations and 30 languages, they highlighted how technology can undermine well-being.

Tristan Harris and Aza Raskin, co-founders of the Center for Humane Technology, are advising global policymakers, heads of state, and national security leaders about the dangers of technology. They have also enlightened millions about these issues and mobilised leaders to tackle technology's adverse effects on society. They are tirelessly raising awareness about the negative impacts of AI on society and actively working with leaders around the world to mitigate its adverse effects.

The crucial point to note here is that while progress promises benefits, unchecked development could undermine human flourishing. We must ensure technology enhances thriving, not imperils it. Lives are at stake, necessitating vigilance, wisdom, and good judgement to guide progress. The path ahead is long, but reason can lead to a sustainable future of prosperity, not ruin, if we start now. Also, the direction we set on right now will be hard to change and therefore, we need to responsibly assess technology's promise of a better world for generations to come. We owe it to future generations to be thoughtful stewards of progress, not just celebrate breakthroughs. Their fate depends on the world we shape today. The responsibility is ours.

The AI Pioneer's Warning: Geoffrey Hinton on Technology's Risks

When Dr Geoffrey Hinton resigned from Google in May 2023, it sent shockwaves through many industries, particularly the AI sector. Geoffrey Everest Hinton, born on December 6, 1947, is a British-Canadian psychologist and computer scientist known for his research on neural networks. From 2013 to 2023, he worked part-time for Google (Google Brain) and the University of Toronto before leaving in May 2023, citing concerns about AI risks. He had initially praised Google for its responsible approach to AI development but altered his perspective after Microsoft integrated a chatbot into Bing. Dr Hinton's resignation from Google reflects concerns about these risks and their societal implications. To fully grasp the various incentives and concerns involved in this situation, we will need to examine the complete story in detail.

In 2017, Dr Hinton co-founded the Vector Institute in Toronto, where he and his graduate students pioneered foundational AI technologies. Recently, Dr Hinton has joined critics in cautioning against the rapid advancement of generative AI, highlighting its potential risks to society. He advocates for developing AI in a way that enhances human flourishing rather than undermining it. He also believes AI has the potential to address humanity's greatest challenges if approached responsibly.

Later, Google acquired Hinton's company for $44 million. Their system enabled increasingly powerful technologies, such as chatbots like ChatGPT and Google Bard. Sutskever became OpenAI's Chief Scientist, and in 2018, Hinton and his long-time collaborators received the Turing Award, known as the 'Nobel of computing,' for their work on neural networks. Around this time, Google, OpenAI, and others built neural networks that could learn from vast amounts of text. Hinton believed that while language understanding and generation were possible, they were inferior to human handling. However, last year, as Google and OpenAI built larger data systems, Hinton's view changed. He still saw the superiority of the human brain in some ways, but the systems were eclipsing human intelligence in others. He said, 'Maybe what is happening in these systems is actually a lot better than the brain.'

Dr Hinton is concerned about the dangers of AI, as he believes it could upend the job market over time, replacing paralegals, assistants, translators, and other jobs. He is also worried about the risks of AI generating its own code and running it, as well as the reality of autonomous weapons. He believes that AI is actually smarter than people, and while many experts believe the threat is hypothetical, he thinks that the race between tech giants like Google and Microsoft is escalating into an unrestrained global race without regulation. Immediate concerns include false photos, videos, and text flooding the internet, making it difficult to discern the truth.

Following the release of OpenAI's new ChatGPT in March, more than 1,000 leaders and researchers signed a letter advocating for a six-month moratorium on new AI systems. They emphasise the profound risks these technologies pose to society and humanity. While technological advancements open new frontiers, responsible stewardship is essential to navigate their impact.

The Urgent Need for Ethical AI and Tech Regulation

Dr Hinton acknowledges that AI progress offers benefits that can improve lives, but he also believes that it poses risks that must be addressed urgently. Unchecked development could undermine humanity, and responsible stewardship is needed to ensure technology fulfils its potential. And while AI enables breakthroughs that improve lives, we must anticipate the dangers of irresponsible use and consequences that are currently beyond our purview.

Put simply, before humanity advances further with AI, it is crucial to carefully consider its costs and ethical responsibilities. Progress should be guided by diligence and wisdom, not just enthusiasm. Only by exercising good judgement can technology's promise be fulfilled without causing harm. Only then can we steer us toward a sustainable future of prosperity and not disaster. We must act now, but we must be proactive rather than reactive. With foresight and compassion, technology can support sustainable progress. We need to understand that this is a completely new paradigm and lives are at stake, and thus, we must embrace responsibility from the start.

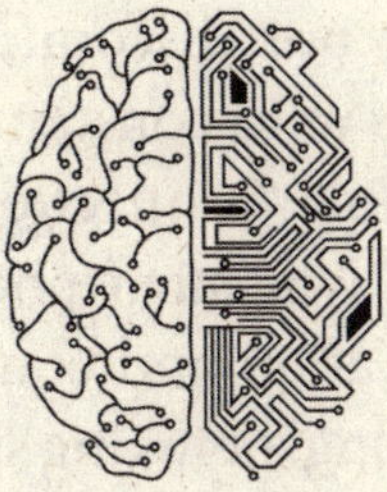

Chapter 15

DIGITAL DETOX

Nomophobia

IN 2016, DR NARENDRA KUMAR PATHAK AT INDIRA GANDHI National Open University noticed a worrying trend. 'We immediately grab our phones upon waking or before sleep,' he stated. 'Checking emails or social media has become a reflex even during ordinary tasks or intimate moments. Smartphones are now so prevalent that being fully present without distractions is challenging.'

Imagine a moment of peace in a public place. How does it feel to not have a screen demanding attention? The truth is that in a culture valuing constant productivity, downtime is often seen as laziness. This societal pressure makes us uncomfortable with solitude, causing us to constantly seek external stimulation instead of embracing introspection. Research shows a strong aversion to boredom and inactivity. Studies led by Tim Wilson reveal that many people would rather experience electric shocks than be left alone with their thoughts, highlighting our discomfort with self-reflection. This discomfort pushes us to constantly engage with devices, missing out on genuine connections and self-discovery. This is also the reason why smartphones are enticing. They provide instant gratification and constant novelty. Whether we are on the move, eating, or taking short breaks, our phones offer an endless stream of information and entertainment, preventing us from being present and truly engaging with our surroundings.

To navigate this digital world, we must reassess our relationship with technology. By creating moments of mindfulness and embracing downtime, we can reclaim opportunities for real connections, creativity, and personal growth. Resisting the urge to constantly check our phones allows us to rediscover the richness of everyday experiences and prioritise meaningful interactions over digital distractions. In the following section, we will explore digital detox tips, the challenges of unplugging, and how to implement these strategies in our lives.

Dr Pathak's Digital Detox Tips for Parents

Studies show people who frequently check their phones experience higher distress during leisure time. Disconnecting can reduce stress, making you feel more connected, rested, and genuinely productive. Though challenging, unplugging can significantly enhance well-being and lead to a richer, more meaningful life.

In his 2016 article. 'Digital Detox in India,' Dr Narendra Kumar Pathak offers a list of crucial pointers for parents aiming to protect their children from digital addiction:

1. Trust Your Instincts and Act Promptly

Parents often have an innate sense when something is wrong. Dr Pathak emphasises that if your instincts suggest a problem, they are probably right. Parents should take a proactive role by monitoring their child's relationship with technology and online behaviour. If something feels off, immediate action is necessary to control digital overuse. Digital detoxing, despite potential resistance, is far better than allowing addiction to take root.

2. Lead by Example

Children mimic their parents' behaviours. Dr Pathak advises parents to set standards by silencing phones during meals, engaging in family conversations, and instituting cyber-free weekends. Consistently demonstrating that family connections take precedence over digital interactions sends a powerful message about real-world relationships' importance.

3. Encourage Real-World Activities

Engage children in outdoor games, sports, cultural travels, and arts to shift focus from the virtual to the real world. Dr Pathak suggests introducing children to enriching activities, making the real world more appealing and less screen dominated.

4. Promote a Tech-Free Bedroom

Good sleep is crucial for cognitive functions like thinking, memorising, and learning. Dr Pathak stresses keeping digital devices out of bedrooms to reinforce the importance of rest. This applies to both children and parents, setting a household standard for technology-free zones at night.

5. **Create a Gadget Inventory**

List all your gadgets to understand technology dependency. Then, list enjoyable activities neglected due to screen time. If the second list is compelling, reclaim those moments from digital distractions.

6. **Set Time Limits**

Allocate specific daily allowances for digital device usage. Restricting screen time frees up space for real-world activities and meaningful social interactions, fostering a more balanced life.

7. **Set Achievable Goals**

Ease into detox by setting realistic targets. Gradually eliminate tech use during certain parts of your day, like lunch breaks or while exercising, rather than making drastic changes.

8. **Change One Habit at a Time**

Don't attempt to ditch all devices simultaneously. Start with one habit, such as banning digital devices during meals or keeping them out of the bedroom. Gradually expand this practice.

9. **Prioritise Sleep**

Ensure good sleep by keeping devices out of the bedroom and avoiding screen time at least two hours before bed. Your bedroom should be a rest sanctuary, not a digital hub.

10. Give Undivided Attention

Practice good manners by fully engaging in face-to-face conversations without phone distractions. This enhances interaction quality and shows respect for those around you.

11. Find a Detox Buddy

Partner with someone on your detox journey. A support system maintains accountability, encourages face-to-face interactions, and keeps you motivated.

12. Leave Gadgets at Home

When walking or running, leave devices behind. Enjoy your surroundings without comparing your life to others on social media. Listen to birds, feel the breeze, and savour the moment.

13. Announce Your Detox

Inform friends and family about your digital detox. Their awareness adds accountability and may inspire them to join, creating a supportive environment.

14. Disable Push Notifications

Reduce smartphone dependency by turning off social media push notifications. Set specific times for checking these apps to regain control over digital habits.

14. Use an Alarm Clock

Replace smartphone alarms with traditional clocks. This prevents early morning screen time, allowing mindful starts to your day.

15. Use Airplane Mode

When jogging or exercising, switch your phone to airplane mode. This helps focus on the activity, reaching a state of relaxation and mindfulness.

16. Gradual Detox

Build up to a full digital detox by incrementally increasing device-free time. Start with 15-minute intervals, gradually extending until you can comfortably unplug for an entire day.

17. Confront Fear of Disconnection

Address out-of-touch fears by informing key contacts of your detox plans. Arrange for someone to handle urgent communications, ensuring peace of mind.

18. Prepare for Temptation

Have engaging activities ready to distract from device-checking urges. Dive into a book, magazine, or hobby to stay occupied.

19. Understand Your Social Media Attraction

Identify why specific sites attract you and find real-world alternatives. Instead of constantly checking your Instagram, visit art galleries or explore nature with friends.

20. Repeat a Mantra

When staying home instead of attending social events, remind yourself, 'Wherever I am is exactly where I need to be.' This combats the fear of missing out and affirms your choices.

21. Creating Your Digital Detox Strategy

Find a strategy tailored to your lifestyle and personality. The goal is to identify naturally rewarding activities that alleviate boredom and anxiety.

22. Connect in Real Life

Positive relationships are key to happiness. Make an effort to interact with people around you, even briefly with a grocery checker or barista at your local cafe.

Overcoming Digital Dependency: Crafting Your Digital Detox Strategy

Unplugging can be tough due to the discomfort that arises when we stop compulsively checking our devices. Many people would rather endure a painful electric shock than face the unease of not checking their devices or feeling unproductive. Thus, we need to have a plan when unplugging in order to keep us on our course. Here's how to create your own digital detox strategy.

Step 1: Create a No-Excuses Plan

1. **Notify Your Circle:** Inform friends, family, and coworkers about your weekend digital detox. This prevents misunderstandings about your lack of response.
2. **Emergency Contact:** Keep an emergency contact during your detox periods. This is more for your peace of mind, ensuring you won't miss urgent matters.
3. **Accountability Buddies:** Enlist friends and family to hold you accountable. Allow them to tease you if you

slip and use social media or send messages, including emails. Think of it as crowd-sourced willpower.

4. **Plan Your Day:** Make specific plans for your unplugged time. This could include activities such as hiking, reading a physical book, practising mindfulness, painting, or simply enjoying nature without electronic distractions.
5. **Analog Tools Ready:** Prepare analogue tools to reduce your reliance on your phone. Print maps, locate a camera, use a traditional alarm clock, and list essential phone numbers. Borrow books from the library or purchase them from a bookstore. Plan for non-digital music options and eliminate unnecessary device use.

Step 2: Hide the Candy

Even with strong willpower, you will need more than determination to unplug. Make reconnecting very inconvenient. These steps may seem extreme but but can assist you on your journey.

1. **Drain Your Batteries:** Let device and computer batteries run out.
2. **Out of Sight:** Put devices and computers out of sight and reach, without chargers.
3. **Separate the Chargers:** Store chargers elsewhere. If temptation is too strong, have someone hide them for you.

This 'out of sight, out of mind' tactic is crucial. Just as you wouldn't carry a bowl of candy everywhere when trying to lose weight, don't keep devices easily accessible during your detox.

Step 3: Natural Rewards for Your Brain

1. **Do Something New and Exciting:** Plan naturally rewarding activities. This eases boredom, anxiety, and restlessness that come with unplugging.
2. **Feel All the Feels:** During a detox, allow yourself to experience all emotions—love, joy, profound gratitude, as well as fear, grief, and frustration. Embracing emotions, even the uncomfortable ones, offers numerous benefits, helping you to stay present.
3. **Embrace Stillness:** When standing in linc, allow yourself to simply be present in the moment, without reaching for distractions. Take this opportunity to observe your surroundings, practice deep breathing, or reflect on your thoughts. This mindful pause can bring a sense of calm and clarity to your day.

Step 4: Remain Consistent and Optimistic

1. **Forgive Yourself:** If you slip up, avoid self-criticism. Remember, lapses are part of the process.
2. **Pre-emptive Comfort:** Find ways to feel safe and secure without sabotaging your detox. This might mean seeking a hug or taking a walk outside.
3. **Identify the Problem:** Determine what caused slip-ups and plan to avoid them next time.
4. **Learn and Adapt:** What will you do differently next time? What have you learnt from your slip up? This can help you optimise your detox strategy.

In conclusion, developing a personalised digital detox strategy is crucial to navigate this discomfort effectively.

By setting clear goals, establishing accountability measures, and preparing alternative activities, you can minimise distractions and regain focus on real-life experiences. Embrace the opportunity to reconnect with yourself and your surroundings, fostering a healthier balance between digital engagement and personal well-being.

Bibliography

The Cyber Effect: A Pioneering Cyber Psychologist Explains How Human Behaviour Changes by Mary Aiken

iBrain: Surviving the Technological Alteration of the Modern by Gary Small

Man Disconnected: How technology has sabotaged what it means to be male by Philip G. Zimbardo

Digital Minimalism in Everyday Life: Overcome Technology Addiction, Declutter Your Mind, and Reclaim our Freedom (Mindfulness and Minimalism Book 1) by James W. Williams

Depth Psychology and the Digital Age by Bonnie Bright

Reclaiming Conversation: The Power of Talk in a Digital Age by Sherry Turkle

Hacker, Hoaxer, Whistleblower, Spy: The Many Faces of Anonymous by Gabriella Coleman

Ethnography and Virtual Worlds: A Handbook of Method by Tom Boellstorff

You Are Not a Gadget by Jaron Lanier

Psychology and the Internet: Intrapersonal, Interpersonal, and Transpersonal Implications by Jayne Gackenbach

Hate Crimes in Cyberspace by Danielle Keats Citron

Cyberpsychology and the Brain: The Interaction of Neuroscience and Affective Computing by Thomas D. Parsons

Ethical Challenges in Digital Psychology and Cyberpsychology by Thomas D. Parsons

Digital Detox: Why Taking a Break from Technology Can Improve Your Well-Being by Bernadette H. Schell

Internet Oligopoly: The Corporate Takeover of Our Digital World by Nikos Smyrnaios

Article on AI by Matthew Urwin (25 Jan 2023, Reviewed by Artem Oppermann)

Acknowledgements

I EXPRESS MY DEEP APPRECIATION TO THE UNSUNG HEROES of society who inspired and motivated me to write *The Human Algorithm*. This book is a tribute to those overlooked, undervalued, and marginalised while many are absorbed in endless scrolling on cell phones. These selfless individuals work tirelessly to make the world better.

I am truly grateful to the wise individuals encountered on this journey, who encouraged thinking outside the box and advocating for unheard voices. We often enjoy privileges at the expense of those lacking the opportunity to shine in well-established fields like arts, literature, science, and others due to lack of support or connections.

Special thanks to Aditya Jairal, editor at Hay House India, for demonstrating genuine character when sincerity is uncommon. Though unknown to him, he showed openness, willingness to respond, read my manuscript, and ultimately publish this book. His support was invaluable in making it a reality.

I also acknowledge the exceptional, yet obscure talents pushed into obscurity today simply for lacking large social media followings. Their abilities deserve recognition and support.

May this book tribute those forgotten souls in this era of distorted truths, where stories masquerade as history and the ill-informed attempt to dictate how we should live. Let us shine a light on individuals standing for humanity, truth, and science, offering unwavering support so they are no longer confined to shadows of obscurity.

Let us embrace a daily detox ritual—placing phones on silent mode, immersing fully in the rich humanity, nature, and truth enveloping us. Instead of mere digital personas, let us participate in heartfelt conversations, truly witnessing others' struggles and triumphs. Deepening empathy, forging authentic connections transcending virtual facades. This deliberate disconnect from digital noise invites quiet reflection and appreciation for profound beauty in genuine human interaction.